HC
470.3
.S93
1986

Szczepanik, Edward
F.

The economic growth
of Hong Kong

$39.75

THE ECONOMIC GROWTH
OF HONG KONG

THE
ECONOMIC GROWTH
OF
HONG KONG

EDWARD SZCZEPANIK

Issued under the auspices of the
Royal Institute of International Affairs

GREENWOOD PRESS, PUBLISHERS
WESTPORT, CONNECTICUT

Library of Congress Cataloging-in-Publication Data

Szczepanik, Edward F.
    The economic growth of Hong Kong.

    Reprint. Originally published: London ; New York :
Oxford University Press, 1958.
    Includes index.
    1. Hong Kong--Economic conditions. I. Title.
HC470.3.S93 1986   330.951'25   85-30507
ISBN 0-313-25054-5 (lib. bdg. : alk. paper)

Reprinted with the permission of The Royal Institute of
International Affairs

Reprinted in 1986 by Greenwood Press
A division of Congressional Information Service, Inc.
88 Post Road West, Westport, Connecticut 06881

Printed in the United States of America

10 9 8 7 6 5 4 3 2 1

TO ANNE

Foreword

BEFORE the war the chief activity of Hong Kong was its entrepôt trade, and this was mainly with China. Today its volume of international trade is considerably greater than before the war, but a much smaller proportion of it is with China and a much larger proportion of its exports consists of local manufactures. There has been a remarkable growth of manufacturing during recent years.

Hong Kong is a very small territory. Its population, now 2½ million, is crowded into 391 square miles of mainly rocky and mountainous land. It has no coal, no oil, no water-power, and hardly any raw materials. Yet it has developed a wide range of manufacturing industries, which employ one-third of its workers and provide exports to the value of £50 million a year.

This spectacular development, which has enabled Hong Kong to achieve standards of living much higher than in most Asian countries, must be of great interest to all who are concerned with problems of economic growth and industrialization. What forms did it take? What conditions made it possible and what forces brought it about? What are the limitations, if any, on further expansion?

These and allied questions are answered by Mr. Szczepanik, a first-class economist who has studied the subject on the spot for four years. His detailed surveys and illuminating analysis make his little book a valuable contribution.

F. BENHAM

Preface

THIS volume is the result of almost four years spent in watching the fascinating industrial revolution in Hong Kong. Professor F. C. Benham was the first to point out that this analysis could be of more than local interest; it could also be an instructive case history to students of economic growth in other countries. Without his encouragement I should probably still be pondering over the mass of collected material and wrestling with the gaps in it. In spite of over a hundred years of the Colony's existence, no study of its economic history has yet been written. This is, therefore, the first attempt to look at Hong Kong's development from a macroeconomic point of view. The method of this study is to concentrate attention on the 1945–55 decade of spontaneous transformation from an entrepôt to an industrial economy. To cope with the statistically almost virgin ground, a lot of spade-work had to be done and often new tools had to be forged. The result is still far from satisfactory, but although the figures presented here may often be burdened with heavy error, they form a consistent macrodynamic picture incorporating both historical and causal factors of growth.

There is a long list of those who helped me in this work and to whom I should like to express my sincere thanks. First of all, my students not only participated in the collection of material but also formed a stimulating audience before which most of the ideas contained in this book were developed. Thanks to the financial support of the University of Hong Kong and of the Royal Institute of International Affairs I was provided with research and clerical assistance. Mr. Poon Kwong Hung, Mr. Ng Kwok Leung, and Miss Mabel Young had in turn their share of duties as research assistants.

Thanks to the exceptional position of Hong Kong as a Far Eastern cross-roads, I enjoyed the opportunity of answering questions from many economists bearing on this study, which helped to formulate my own views. I am especially grateful to Dr. P. N. Rosenstein-Rodan for his stimulating influence. Throughout the whole period of study I had to rely on the generous advice and criticism offered by Professor E. S. Kirby and Mr. J. J. Cowperthwaite. Mrs. Ruth Kirby went over the whole manuscript and did much to improve its form. The index was made by Mrs. B. M. D. Smith. My wife acted as the chief, severe, and unremitting critic. All the deficiencies left are, of course, entirely my own.

E. S.

University of Hong Kong,
Hong Kong B.C.C.
April 1957

Contents

IV. DYNAMIC BALANCE-SHEET

STATISTICAL APPENDIX

Contents

GRAPHS

MAP

I
AN OUTLINE

I

The Riddle of Growth Acceleration

THE first hundred years of the British Crown Colony of Hong Kong may be described as a century of the growth of an entrepôt economy. This phase ended with the outbreak of the Pacific War and the occupation of Hong Kong by Japan in 1941. On 30 August 1945, when Hong Kong was liberated after four years of occupation, its economy was in ruins. The population was reduced to about one-third of its pre-war size; entrepôt trade, which formerly provided the main source of the national income, had dwindled to nothing; industry was at a standstill, houses were destroyed or dilapidated. Ten years later, the Colony achieved the fame of being one of the most prosperous territories in the Far East. This was due to the remarkable transformation of Hong Kong from a trading into an industrial economy, for the entrepôt trade was never restored to its pre-war relative significance. The rapid economic growth which was the outcome of this process made possible the absorption during a decade of a population increase to at least 400 per cent. above the 1945 level. It is difficult to find a comparable example in the rate of recovery and acceleration of economic growth. The question which immediately arises is how to explain this fascinating case of economic development. To answer this question and to present the mechanism of growth in historical and analytical terms is the purpose of this book.

1. Advantages of location have undoubtedly been at work in Hong Kong, situated as it is at a cross-roads of major oceanic routes and on one of the best natural harbours. This last factor explains why long ago Hong Kong had already surpassed the older, neighbouring, Portuguese colony of Macao, which throughout the seventeenth and eighteenth centuries was the chief port for Western trade with China. Whereas Macao was at one time an ideal port for the comparatively shallow-draught vessels of olden days, the coming of the modern vessel proved to be a severe blow to its trade, which moved mainly to Hong Kong.

B

On the other hand, advantages of location do not differ very much nowadays if comparison is made, say, between Hong Kong and Singapore. Moreover, if due account is taken of the greater relative scarcity of land for cultivation, housing, and industrial purposes resulting mainly from the hilly terrain, Hong Kong will be found to be in a less advantageous position. Economic development in Hong Kong had to reckon with the costly process of reclaiming land from the sea (even for the construction of the new airport), breaking new roads through hard rocks, and forming sites by systematic levelling of hills. Furthermore, the construction of reservoirs in order to overcome the acute shortage of water in Hong Kong was a much more costly solution than laying down pipes conducting water from the mainland, which was possible in Singapore. In spite of these disadvantages, and starting with a similar entrepôt-economy basis, post-war industrialization in Hong Kong was quicker, more diversified, and on a larger scale than in Singapore.

The mineral wealth of Hong Kong is almost negligible, although existing resources are intensively exploited and geological research continues, recently bringing the discovery of graphite and beryl. But the absence of raw materials and sources of energy of almost any kind did not prevent Hong Kong from developing a wide range of manufacturing industries and surpassing in this respect many Far Eastern countries better equipped with natural resources.

2. If the first of the classical factors of production, land, was not primarily responsible for the acceleration of Hong Kong's economic growth, what was the contribution of the second 'original' factor, labour? There is no doubt that here lies at least part of the clue. Hong Kong has enjoyed the benefit of possessing a hard-working and intelligent Chinese labour force. These qualities deserve special stress. But, again, the Chinese constitute the bulk of the population in Singapore and Macao, not to speak of Mainland China and Taiwan (Formosa).

As far as Singapore and Macao are concerned, the difference consists in the historical structure of the Chinese population. In both these ports the Chinese are descendants of settlers who gradually trickled away from their native villages as farmers, fishermen, craftsmen, or merchants. In Hong Kong, on the other hand, there has been, after the war, a powerful injection of new labour from the Mainland, under pressure of political events. They came in bulk, frightened by Communism and prepared to work hard rather than live under terror again.

A similar bulk injection was received simultaneously by Taiwan, but its racial and social composition was different. The newcomers to Taiwan, who came from various provinces of China, had difficulty in merging with the predominantly Fukienese indigenous population, speaking a different language and thinking in different political terms. In Hong Kong, on the other hand, the majority of refugees came from Kwangtung, the same province as the permanent residents of the Colony, both groups mixing easily with each other. Other groups, such as those who came from Shanghai, formed almost entirely new social strata in Hong Kong, e.g. artists, scholars, and, of special importance to us, an industrial entrepreneurial class. Moreover, the refugees who went to Taiwan were mainly politicians, soldiers, and bureaucrats of the Kuomintang régime. It was a group ready to rule or fight but not to work. Refugees in Hong Kong were determined to survive through toil.

3. During the post-war decade the capital supply in Hong Kong was certainly favouring rapid economic growth. Refugees from China seldom came with empty hands. Capital not only accompanied and followed but often preceded the streams of refugees. The Korean War, in spite of political tension, did not drive much capital out from Hong Kong, and speculative gains contributed to local capital formation. The war in Indochina brought about another wave of refugee capital attracted by investment prospects in Hong Kong. Recently, political unrest and tension in Singapore and Malaya produced similar effects. Absence of restrictions on transfer and convertibility has attracted capital also from more distant Asian countries.

Apart from the inflow of capital from outside, an important source of capital formation in Hong Kong was provided by internal savings, both private and public. Chinese people are not only hard-working and intelligent; they are also very thrifty. Part of these private savings goes abroad, as aid to families left in poverty in China. The rest, however, is retained in the Colony, and usually it is invested directly in tools and even small machinery. In addition to individual private savings, corporate savings were also forthcoming. Finally, the role of public savings cannot be minimized. The Government has managed to build up substantial capital reserves from annual budgetary surpluses, which have been partly used to finance public-works projects: roads, water reservoirs, the new airport, ferry piers, market installations, schools, hospitals, &c. Among these projects, the resettlement by the end of 1956 of about 100,000 refugees in houses constructed by the Government deserves particular stress.

Compared with the influx of private capital from abroad and the process of internal capital formation, the role of grants of about HK$20 million from the Colonial Development and Welfare Fund during the decade becomes almost insignificant. There has been no aid to Hong Kong under the Colombo Plan, or under any other international-aid scheme. Even foreign aid to refugees was not very large, in spite of various international appeals, although mention should be made of the American grants-in-aid to numerous charitable organizations helping the refugees.

4. It is difficult to separate 'entrepreneurship' in Hong Kong from capital and, often, from labour. Most of the newly created industrial enterprises are small family concerns, combining entrepreneurship with capital and labour. In larger industrial firms, at least the unity of entrepreneurship with capital ownership is preserved, partnerships and private-company firms being the predominant ones. In spite of the two factors being indistinguishable, it is important to stress that Chinese entrepreneurship is of high calibre. The Chinese entrepreneur is ready to assume risks, explore new markets, and experiment with new products, raw materials, and production techniques. In Schumpeterian terms, he is indeed an innovator.

Much of this important entrepreneurial skill arrived in Hong Kong from Shanghai and Canton. With Chinese entrepreneurs came also numerous entrepreneurs of European descent. A situation was thus created where, to use Rostow's expression, an entrepreneurial *élite* appeared in Hong Kong almost overnight.[1] Combined with an excellent labour force and fairly rich sources of capital supply, this *élite* helped enormously to

[1] W. W. Rostow, 'The Take-Off into Self-sustained Growth', *Econ. J.*, March 1956, p. 42.

lay down the foundations for a spectacular industrial development.

5. The above considerations seem to bring us very near to solving, in general terms, the riddle of the recent economic growth of Hong Kong. The answer would not be complete, however, if we did not take into account a whole complex set of institutional factors, among which good government should perhaps be placed first. British colonial administration contributed a great deal towards creating an atmosphere conducive to the steady economic expansion of Hong Kong. Connected with this are the advantages resulting from imperial preference and sterling area membership.

Laissez-faire capitalism is another institutional datum of the utmost importance for understanding the recent growth of Hong Kong's economy. The Colony was founded as a free port and this idea has remained almost unchanged. Economic liberalism extends, of course, not only to foreign trade but also to all internal economic activities: production, transport, exchange, and finance. The economic development of Hong Kong has not been directed by any over-all national plans. Instead of appeals to national pride or imposition of overriding national aims to benefit future generations, self-interest has been the prime mover of Hong Kong's economic growth. Even the growth of trade unionism did not produce any significant change in the functioning of capitalism in Hong Kong. Strikes, mounting wage claims, &c. were seldom employed by trade unions in the Colony. This can be explained partially by a large proportion of non-unionized labour and partially by the political division of the unions between those who favour the Nationalists and those who support the Communists, which results in a considerable weakening of the whole power of trade unions.

Other elements of institutional character, such as the Chinese social structure, which presents a close network of families, clans, secret societies, religious sects, professional, cultural, or charitable organizations, as well as various deep-rooted traits of ancient Chinese philosophy—all would have to be included in a complete analysis of Hong Kong's recent economic growth. These factors, however, belong to a realm beyond the reach of the crude tools which an economist has been trained to handle.

6. An answer to the question how to explain the post-war acceleration of the rate and the change in the character of economic growth of Hong Kong cannot be given, therefore, by pointing to one specific element. The case presents an almost unique combination of a number of basic developmental factors: good location, cheap and skilled labour, adequate supply of capital, and excellent entrepreneurship.

Looking at the case from a historical point of view, the elements which stimulated Hong Kong's industrial revolution can be classified as follows: (*a*) flexible institutional framework within which a responsive infrastructure could develop; (*b*) violent population pressure and the resulting bulk injection of excellent labour, capital, and entrepreneurship; (*c*) absence of opportunities for any substantial development of primary industries; (*d*) decline in the traditional source of income generation which consisted in entrepôt trade.

A systematic examination of these factors will be carried out in the first part of this book.

The subsequent part of the study will be devoted to the analysis of the interplay of these institutional and historical factors with the causal elements in the spontaneous growth of manufacturing industry.

In the concluding chapter an attempt will be made to examine the growth of the economy as a whole in terms of dynamic economics and to give an outline of the prospects concerning future development.

II
THE ENTREPÔT ECONOMY

2

The Institutional Framework

ECONOMIC SYSTEM OF HONG KONG

HONG KONG is often described as an outpost of Western civilization in an Oriental setting. From the economic point of view, this implies the Western capitalist system infused with numerous specifically Chinese elements.

An economic system is defined as the totality of inter-dependent units of economic decisions.[1] In the capitalist system of Hong Kong, the two main types of such units are households and private business enterprises which are very often organized on a family basis. Public agencies also exist, but they play a com-paratively small economic role. Even the public-utility enter-prises are mainly privately owned. But, whereas the role of public agencies is small, the importance of households cannot be neglected. Large sections of the population still rely on pro-duction of goods and services within households. This is not only the case among the 'boat people', where whole families spend most of their life on junks, but also among the agri-cultural population, and often in commerce, handicrafts, and even industry, especially textiles and plastics. The capitalist economy of Hong Kong contains, therefore, numerous elements of a domestic system mitigating some of the evils of com-petitive capitalism.

With the exception of land, which is Crown property, and a few monopolies, there are no restrictions on the scope of the institution of private ownership, and the institution of in-heritance is relatively little hampered by succession (estate) duties. Centralized economic planning is almost unknown in Hong Kong. The few instances of planning by means of ration-ing, licensing, or exchange control had to be introduced by the Government only because of external political developments. The Government has as its main objectives only the aiding and

[1] O. Lange, 'The Scope and Method of Economics', *R. Econ. Stud.*, vol. 13, 1945–6.

promoting of private enterprises by land reclamation, irrigation, supply of water, building and maintenance of roads, dissemination of information, &c., thus securing the basic prerequisites of an orderly competition which is the main driving force in a capitalist system.

Is the economic system existing in Hong Kong good or bad? [1] An ideal economic system has not yet been invented, hence the Hong Kong system must have its merits and demerits. On the other hand, as value judgements are not the province of an economist, it is impossible to decide with the aid of purely economic considerations whether this system, on balance, has more advantages or vice versa. Assuming, however, certain accepted social ends, it is possible to indicate which of them are most likely to be achieved in a given economy and which are incompatible with the existing system.

It is convenient in this type of discussion to distinguish the following goals commonly accepted, at least in the West: maximization of national income; minimization of distributive differences; stabilization of the rate of income growth; freedom in the choice of occupation, in income disbursement, and in the acquisition of property, normally defined as 'economic freedom'. Let us examine in turn the methods by which the Hong Kong economic system achieves these social aims.

Not all the conditions of income-maximization, i.e. full employment of all resources combined with the most efficient methods of production, exist in Hong Kong. First of all, human labour resources are not fully employed, but this can be explained mainly by the influx of refugees from the mainland of China.[2] Another reason is, however, inherently connected with the working of the capitalist system; it has no automatic device to secure employment of all those willing to work, even at a certain minimum, socially-accepted level of wages.

Secondly, it is difficult to say whether the most efficient methods of production are used in Hong Kong. The criteria of efficiency are different here from those of the West. With plentiful cheap labour, the most efficient, from the economic

---

[1] For a more detailed examination of this question, see the present writer's article on the 'Economic System of Hong Kong', *Far East. Econ. R.*, 28 October 1954.

[2] See below, Chapter 3.

point of view, are labour-absorbing methods, and these are extensively used in Hong Kong. On the other hand, unrestricted competitive capitalism implies the existence of a great number of small productive units which not only cannot benefit from the economies of large-scale production, but also are unable to derive all the advantages arising from the division of labour. The principle of private ownership prevails; this, on the whole, is an element securing a high level of efficiency. Many enterprises are family concerns. In most cases this eliminates much bureaucratic wastefulness, facilitates supervision, secures continuity, and contributes towards harmony in industrial relations built on family ties.[1]

Capitalism has no inherent tendency towards the equalization of incomes. The principle of free entry into every line of production provides an important safety-valve, but its significance diminishes in view of the inequalities at the start resulting from the institution of private ownership and inheritance. There is, therefore, a great inequality in the distribution of income in Hong Kong. The bulk of the population is living on earnings not exceeding HK$300 per month per household. According to my estimate,[2] this section of the population constitutes about 95 per cent. of the total population, and it is receiving only 60 per cent. of the national income. This is a striking figure, which is largely due to the pressure of refugees on the level of earnings in the Colony. But it is also inherently connected with the operation of the capitalist system. Here, perhaps, lies its main fault.

Another important disadvantage of capitalism in Hong Kong consists in the fluctuating level of national income. Periods of prosperity and depression are inevitable in an unplanned capitalist system. On the whole, they are considered undesirable, but it is hard to see how they can be avoided in an economy depending to such an extent on external forces, unlikely to be controlled even under planning. The capitalist system, possessing a safety-valve in the shape of the cancellation of the errors of optimism and pessimism, is probably more suitable for Hong Kong than any other. Hong Kong's lack of

---

[1] See below, Chapter 6.
[2] R. A. Ma and E. F. Szczepanik, *The National Income of Hong Kong 1947–1950* (Hong Kong Univ. Press, 1955), pp. 11–12.

internal natural resources and consequent dependence on the marginal demand in its markets and fluctuating export opportunities are the obvious reasons for reliance on capitalism as the best system for this type of economy.

Finally, another major social aim is that of economic freedom. It is here that the advantages of the capitalist system are most obvious. Capitalism secures the consumer's sovereignty, freedom in the choice of occupation, in the disposal of an individual's income, and in the acquisition, possession, and transfer of property. For people cherishing these ideas, Hong Kong still holds great opportunities. Almost all kinds of goods the world can supply are available in Hong Kong. There is freedom in the choice of employer and of the kind of job. Even compulsory service in the armed forces does not apply to the local Chinese population.[1] Individual ability, skill, and training are the main considerations in the labour market. Taxation is low, and what the population earns can be turned into the channels regarded as the most worth-while: sometimes it is hoarding diamonds or playing mah-jong; but more often a coolie or a rickshaw-puller saves his cents for the purpose of becoming a farmer when he retires; an ex-hawker becomes a money-lender charging exorbitant interest rates even to his friends; and almost everybody dreams of the possibility of making a good deal in an import–export transaction, thus both enriching himself and performing the useful function of an entrepôt merchant. In this way some fabulous fortunes have been accumulated in Hong Kong and retained within the family circle. These families are producing great philanthropists, sponsors of the arts and science, promoters of new industries, founders of new agricultural communities, and great social benefactors mitigating some of the undesirable effects of the capitalist system, which to some people often allocates a tragically meagre portion.

ECONOMIC ROLE OF THE GOVERNMENT

Politically speaking, Hong Kong is a British Crown Colony which was created primarily for economic reasons. The main aim of the Letters Patent issued by Queen Victoria on 5 April

[1] National service is, in theory, compulsory for all British subjects, irrespective of race; in practice, compulsion is only applied to those who claim British nationality, as Chinese may retain Chinese nationality.

1843 was to establish on a barren, rocky island a settlement of British merchants, devoting their resources and skill to the promotion of British trade relations with China.[1] These merchants had no interest in power politics, nor had they leisure, ability, or resources to solve the problems of the defence, police, justice, and routine administration of a new community. All this had to be provided or organized by the home country. In the course of time, the basic idea of a division of labour between a group of adventurous merchants and the rest of the British community living in the far distant isles has perhaps been blurred, and with the growth of the Colony's population it began to lose its significance and justification. Nevertheless, it is still the underlying politico-economic principle of the Government.

The main characteristics of this system of government consist in the fact that legislative decisions and the chief administrative offices are not left with members of the Colony's community but with persons selected for this purpose by the home Government. Similarly, the bulk of the defence duties is undertaken by the members of the home society. Local government, in the sense of autonomous administrative units, does not exist in Hong Kong. The Urban Council does not have the municipal functions usually associated with its name. It has no revenue from rates or taxes; its expenditure is regulated as that of a government department, as it simply replaced the Sanitary Board in 1935 and mainly carries out its duties. The administration of the New Territories [2] is also only a government department in the charge of a District Commissioner.

The Governor, appointed by the Sovereign, is the supreme authority in the Colony. He rules with the help of the Executive Council and various government departments. The Legislative Council advises the Governor, and its consent is always asked for laws and for the approval of government expenditure, but all its members are appointed. Most of the members of the Executive Council sit on the Legislative Council. This system of government results in a high degree of concentration of authority, which, on the one hand, secures great administrative

---

[1] Sir C. Collins, *Public Administration in Hong Kong* (London, RIIA and IPR, 1952), p. 46.

[2] Leased from China in 1898 for ninety-nine years.

efficiency but, on the other, differs considerably from the Western systems of government. A list of less than twenty names would suffice to include all those who have most influence in government, finance, and big business in Hong Kong. But although Hong Kong is run as a business concern 'it is a very well-run department store—with welfare services and all'.[1]

Tables 1 and 2 (pp. 149–50), illustrate the general pattern of governmental spending and financing during 1952–6, i.e. the main period of industrial take-off.[2] It appears from the analysis of these tables that the economic role of the Government of Hong Kong consists mainly in the provision of various economic and social services to the community at large. The maintenance of routine administration, law, order, and defence come next, forming together about 40 per cent. of total expenditure. This order may be regarded as reflecting the 'scale of priorities' of the Government. In view of the political organization of the Colony, it is difficult to say to what extent this scale may also reflect the preferences of the Colony's population taken as a whole.

Although the pattern of public spending in 1952–6 was fairly rigid, there was one significant change, an increase in the proportion of expenditure on economic and social services, and a corresponding reduction of expenditure on administration, maintenance of law and order, and defence. This is indicated in Table 3 (p. 151).

The Government is financing its activities mainly with the aid of tax-revenue, collected at a relatively moderate burden to the community and with the help of government trading.[3] The three largest items producing tax revenue are earnings and profits tax, the import duty on tobacco, and rates.

Earnings and profits tax, which is a substitute for the more orthodox type of income tax, was first imposed in 1947. The standard rate was 10 per cent. until 1950–1, when it was raised to the present level of $12\frac{1}{2}$ per cent. The tax falls into the following four categories:

---

[1] H. Ingrams, *Hong Kong*, London, HMSO, 1952, pp. 234–5.

[2] This analysis is an extension of my article on 'The Economic Role of the Government of Hong Kong', *Far East. Econ. R.*, 11 November 1954.

[3] The burden of taxation in Hong Kong is estimated at 8–9 per cent. of the national income (Ma and Szczepanik, *National Income*, p. 13).

1. Profits Tax (sub-divided into a Corporation Profits Tax and a Business Profits Tax), charged at the standard rate on all companies or businesses operating in the Colony. In the case of unincorporated businesses, no tax is payable provided their profits do not exceed $7,000.

2. Salaries Tax, charged on all individuals in receipt of income from employment. This is charged at graduated rates, ranging from one-fifth of the standard rate on the first $5,000 of net chargeable income, to double the standard rate on net chargeable income exceeding $45,000. In arriving at net chargeable income the following allowances are first deducted: (*a*) personal allowance $7,000; (*b*) allowance for wife $7,000; (*c*) child allowance, ranging from $2,000 for the first child to $200 for the ninth child. There are also insurance allowances. The maximum charge, however, is limited to tax at the standard rate on the total assessable income without the deduction of any allowances.

3. Interest Tax, charged at the standard rate on most interest payments.

4. Property Tax, charged at half the standard rate on the net rateable value of all land and buildings in the Colony.[1]

Of these four categories, the most productive is the profits tax, which in 1954–5 formed 75 per cent. of the total revenue from the earnings and profits tax, the rest being formed by the property tax (11 per cent.), salaries and personal tax (11 per cent.), and interest tax (3 per cent.).

In addition to the above taxes, there is estate duty, charged at between 2 and 52 per cent., and rates, which have been levied in the Colony since 1845, and amount now to 17 per cent. p.a. of rateable value in Hong Kong Island and Kowloon, and 11 per cent. in the New Territories. There is no general tariff, and for most goods the Colony remains a free port. Import duties are levied, however, on locally consumed liquor, tobacco, hydrocarbon oils, toilet preparations and proprietary medicines, and table waters. Stamp duties, entertainment tax, bets and sweeps tax, business registration tax, meals and liquors tax, and dance halls tax exhaust the list of taxes. The remainder of government revenue is derived from the fees of court or office, licences, fines, forfeitures, and royalties, as well as from such trading activities as the lease, rent, and sale of land, the post office, water supply, and the Kowloon–Canton Railway.

[1] *Hong Kong Annual Report 1955*, p. 43.

Financing by loans has been carried out on a very small scale,[1] and the use of the money-printing machine is practically unknown. In the post-war period the Government has been able—even though unintentionally—to accumulate considerable surpluses and thus create substantial reserve funds. Table 4 (p. 151) illustrates the growth of public revenue and expenditure and the process of accumulation of budgetary surpluses.

On 31 March 1955 surplus balances, apart from other reserve funds, amounted to HK$372 million, which was the equivalent of one year's expenditure. Most of these reserves are invested in sterling securities. The disposal of these surpluses is a matter of great interest. Public works and the extension of social services seem to provide the most natural outlet. There are indications that this is the general line of the economic policy of the Government. Three major projects alone, namely Tai Lam Chung Water Reservoir, Kai Tak Airport, and Kowloon Hospital, are absorbing more than HK$250 million from the accumulated and current surpluses. Every year public expenditure on the Colony's infrastructure [2] is increasing. Among the most recent public works, mention should be made of a large reclamation, covering 227 acres at Kun Tong, to supply factory sites for the Colony's rapidly increasing industries.

THE SUPPLY OF MONEY

Absence of economic controls, so conspicuous in the field of foreign trade and fiscal policy, extends also to the monetary field in Hong Kong. The present monetary system dates back to 1935, when the sterling-exchange standard was formally introduced and the approximate exchange rate of HK$1 = 1s. 3d. (or £1 = HK$16) was established. This is actually the rate quoted to the International Monetary Fund in 1947 as par, and also used in government accounts, but the banks may deal with the public at a few points on either side of this rate, both to allow for a profit margin, and, to a slight extent, to meet

---

[1] During the post-war period, only one loan (3½ per cent. Rehabilitation Loan of HK$50 million) was raised by the Government, in 1947–8.

[2] The term 'infrastructure' is used in this study to denote 'social overhead capital'.

fluctuations in demand and supply. The Hong Kong dollar is the direct descendant of the silver Mexican dollar which was the first legal tender in the Colony.[1] The present legal tender is the one-dollar note issued by the Government. There is no central bank in the Colony, but three private banks have the right of issuing bank-notes under separate ordinances or under a Royal Charter (the Chartered Bank). In addition the Government also issues coins and small subsidiary notes. All notes issued have 100 per cent. backing in sterling held by the Exchange Fund.

Most of the bank-notes (about 95 per cent.) are issued by the Hongkong & Shanghai Banking Corporation. The Chartered Bank comes next, followed by the Mercantile Bank of India with only a very small issue. The note issue, including duress notes, at the beginning of 1946 was about HK$400 million, and at the end HK$459 million, i.e. HK$59 million was added to the currency issue in the year 1946. This figure rose to HK$675 million in 1947, HK$783 million in 1948, and from this time onwards it remained at a remarkably stable level of about HK$800 million. The supply of government notes and coins was also very stable, at about HK$40 million, bringing the total of cash supply to HK$840–850 million. Table 5 (p. 152) illustrates the composition of the total supply of cash in Hong Kong in 1950–6.

The only significant change during this six-year period was a slight reduction in the issue of bank-notes by the Hongkong & Shanghai Banking Corporation in 1955, which should be regarded as a reflection of the shortage of sterling in the Colony, the attempts at credit contraction in 1955,[2] and the rise in the bank rate in the United Kingdom which attracted some funds from Hong Kong. With this exception, the rigidity of the currency supply during the period of industrial expansion was remarkable. This was a factor contributing to the stability of the general level of prices in the Colony throughout the whole

---

[1] A full description and history of the monetary system of Hong Kong is given by F. H. H. King in *The Monetary System of Hong Kong* (Hong Kong, K. Weiss, 1953); see also G. B. Endacott, 'The Currency Problem in Early Hong Kong'; 'The Hong Kong Mint and the Colony's Currency Problem', *Far East. Econ. R.*, 19 and 26 April, 14 and 21 May 1956; and E. S. Kirby, 'Money, Banking, and the Stock Exchange in Hong Kong', ibid. 15 December 1955.

[2] See below, p. 23.

C

post-war period, as shown by the following statistics of the general retail price index (annual average; March 1947 = 100).[1]

1947	1948	1949	1950	1951	1952	1953	1954	1955	1956
94	93	104	109	119	120	121	118	115	118

A complete analysis of the role of monetary factors would still require an examination of the supply of bank money. In addition to the above-mentioned three banks enjoying the right of issue, there are in Hong Kong over ninety licensed banks, most of which belong to a clearing-house association.[2] In the absence of bank-deposits statistics, the only data which can throw some light on the supply of bank money are the clearing-house figures, which were as follows:

(HK$ 'ooo million)

1947	1948	1949	1950	1951	1952	1953	1954	1955	1956
6·6	8·3	11·0	14·4	18·0	14·3	12·4	13·4	14·0	15·0

It would be difficult to find in the above statistics an indication that a credit expansion was practised by the Colony's banks during the period 1950–6.[3] There are, however, other reasons to believe that the banks had some responsibility for the Stock Exchange inflation in this period.

There is one further line of analysis, unexplored up to now, which could provide additional information concerning the supply of bank money during Hong Kong's industrial expansion. Besides the licensed banks, the Colony contains a great number of unlicensed 'native' banks. They are called *Ngan Ho*

[1] E. F. Szczepanik, *The Cost of Living in Hong Kong* (Hong Kong Univ. Press, 1956), p. 19.

[2] At the end of 1955 there were 91 licensed banks, of which 33 were authorized to deal in foreign exchange, and 51 belonged to the Clearing House Association located at the Hongkong & Shanghai Banking Corporation.

[3] The clearing figures do not include internal transfers between the accounts held by the Hongkong & Shanghai Banking Corporation, which is the largest holder of deposits in the Colony. The increase in the 1951 clearing-house figures was due to the trade boom caused by the Korean War.

(or *Chin Jon*), and although not officially recognized as banks, they are normally members of the Chinese Gold & Silver Exchange. Their chief sources of income are remittances to China and speculation in gold and in foreign bank-notes, for which the Gold & Silver Exchange is the market. As a sideline, these banks undertake some lending. The credit channels provided by native banks are, however, mainly confined to mortgage transactions within a small circle of relatives, close friends, and associated firms. The general public has practically no access to these channels. Within the Chinese social structure, however, these banks perform a very important role. There are good reasons to believe that speculative profits made by them helped to some extent in financing a number of small-scale industrial enterprises in Hong Kong in the post-war period. Unfortunately, quantitative evaluation is impossible.

We may thus summarize this discussion by stating that the Colony's licensed banks preserved their traditional 'commercial' character without venturing to enter the field of industrial financing to any significant extent. Absence of information prevents us from estimating the size of credit provided by native banks, but it seems unlikely that their loans were considerable. There are, therefore, reasons to believe that the rigidity of supply of cash and bank money was an important element contributing towards internal price-stability. This, and the resulting stability of the value of the HK dollar, produced a favourable 'monetary climate' for the growth of new industrial enterprises.

THE CAPITAL MARKET

A highly differentiated capital market has been a distinctive feature of Hong Kong. The character of the Colony as a trading port necessitated the development of a credit system linking retailers with wholesalers, and wholesalers with godowns, storage, docks, and shipping companies. Connected with warehousing was the provision of mortgage credit against the goods stored. Finally, the inherent risks gave rise to a considerable insurance business, which in turn provided channels for financing some investment in housing, and perhaps also in certain industrial enterprises although on a rather limited scale.

Most Hong Kong firms, both commercial and industrial,

started as modest ventures of single proprietors, gradually changing into a partnership and sometimes into a private company. The public-company form has never been common in the Colony. Thus the original capital normally had to be provided from the founders' past personal savings, supplemented perhaps by a loan from friends or relatives. The expansion of the firm depended subsequently on the volume of profits ploughed back and on the credit provided by banks, wholesalers, docks, and godowns. The nature of this credit, as well as the legal character of Hong Kong's firms, make any quantitative analysis of this part of the capital market almost impossible.

The financing of the relatively small number of firms organized as public companies is reflected in Stock Exchange dealings. The number of securities quoted on the Hong Kong Stock Exchange [1] fluctuates between seventy and eighty titles, but dealings are confined mainly to about twenty securities. The following statistics show the volume of business recorded in the Exchange in 1948–56.[2]

(HK$ million)

1948	1949	1950	1951	1952	1953	1954	1955	1956
159	88	60	141	142	151	252	333	211

During the post-war period annual yield from local shares varied from 6 to 8 per cent. when the political situation was regarded as secure, and from 10 to 20 per cent. when rumours spread that the future of Hong Kong was threatened. Thus the market acts as a political barometer for the Far East.[3] Investment in industrial shares became clearly accentuated for the first time in 1952. As the commodities market was unfavourable,

[1] It had its beginning in the institution founded in 1891 under the name of the Hong Kong Stock Exchange. In 1921 the Hong Kong Sharebrokers' Association was founded by dealers who could not join the Exchange as members. During the Japanese occupation the official market was closed. When it was re-opened (in March 1948) the two institutions were already amalgamated (in 1947) into the new Hong Kong Stock Exchange. As there is no legal obligation to deal in shares through the Exchange, there are also a great number of unregistered brokers.

[2] Figures compiled from *Far East. Econ. R.*

[3] For a historical treatment of the Hong Kong stock market, see Szczepanik, 'Financing the Post-war Economic Growth of Hong Kong', ibid., 20 December 1956.

gold speculation and real estate investment were unattractive, and private mortgage credit found only narrow outlets, idle money began to look for income by investment in industrial shares. This tendency continued in 1953, when the yields reached 10–12 per cent. for industrials, 8–9 per cent. for utilities, and 6–8 per cent. for real estate. In 1954 the situation in the Hong Kong shares market improved further. After its flight in 1952–3 capital began to return from unprofitable adventures abroad. This gave rise to a large demand for utilities as well as other shares, so that average annual yields fell to 6–7 per cent. A minor boom prevailed in the market in 1955, when local idle money and foreign capital flooded it and prices went up under speculative influences. As a result, the volume of transactions on the Stock Exchange in 1955 reached the highest post-war peak, about HK$333 million, i.e. more than double the 1948 level. This speculative tendency was stopped by an increase in the rate of interest on overdrafts in August 1955, and by further credit restrictions imposed by leading banks of the Colony in November 1955.

The Exchange enables dealings to be carried out in the shares of the Hongkong & Shanghai Banking Corporation, the Bank of East Asia, and the three largest Hong Kong insurance companies: Union Insurance, Lombard Insurance, and China Underwriters. Public capital absorbed by these insurance companies is, in turn, invested by them in local government loans, bonds, debentures, shares, house property, as well as in industry of the Colony.[1] The importance of capital provided by the insurance companies could properly be appreciated if we added to the above list other insurance enterprises which are private companies, and the local finance and investment companies, whose shares are not quoted on the Stock Exchange but who contribute considerably to the provision of industrial and other capital in the Colony. In 1955–6 only three investment companies (Allied Investors, Yangtsze Finance, and Hongkong & Far East Investment Co.) had their shares quoted on the Stock Exchange.

Apart from insurance companies, direct investment in real property and hotels is open via the Stock Exchange channels through the shares of Hongkong Realties, Hongkong Land

[1] Approximately 10 per cent. of this capital was invested in house property.

Investment Co., Chinese Estates, Humphrey, and Hongkong & Shanghai Hotels. Several shipping companies (Eastern Asia Navigation Co., Wheelock Marden Group, Indochina Navigation Co., United Waterboats) as well as docks, wharves, and godowns (Hongkong & Kowloon Wharves, Hongkong Docks, China Provident) also offer opportunities for investment by the general public through the Stock Exchange. This helped in the development of the port, its facilities, and shipping. But the most active part of the stock market is formed by dealings in local public-utility shares: Hongkong Tramways, Peak Tramway, Star Ferry, Yaumati Ferry, China Light & Power Co., Hongkong Electric Co., and Hong Kong Telephone Co. It is in this way that the Stock Exchange provides smooth channels to finance a great part of the Colony's infrastructure. However, even in this case the reliance on traditional private-finance sources is clearly marked; such enterprises as the two motor-bus companies are not open to public investors.

Only a very limited number of industries avail themselves of the Stock Exchange channels. Shares listed on the Exchange include among 'Industrials' Cements, HK Ropes, and Metal Industries; and among 'Cottons' Wing On Textiles, Textile Corporation, and Nanyang Mills. This supports the thesis that the bulk of the capital financing the development of manufacturing industry in Hong Kong came from private sources through direct investment channels. Contrasted with this, 'Stores' and 'Miscellaneous', i.e. companies representing mainly commercial interests, occupy a much more prominent place on the Stock Exchange lists. But none of the large export houses of the Colony, such as Jardine, Matheson, Butterfield & Swire, or J. D. Hutchison, figure on the Stock Exchange list. All of them are private companies or partnerships. This shows that the traditions of private financing extended from the entrepôt trade to the field of manufacturing industry. But the role of such companies has been to float and manage public corporations rather than to carry out ventures on their own.

3

Population Pressure

THE last official census in Hong Kong took place in 1931. The total number of persons living in the Colony at that time was 840,000 (rounded figure, excluding military personnel).[1] Between 1937 and 1939 there was an influx of 600,000–700,000 persons, brought about by the Sino-Japanese War. As a result, the pre-war population peak was reached in 1940 at the level of about 1·8 million. After 1940 the population began to flow back to China, and in March 1941, according to an unofficial census made by the air-raid wardens, the population was estimated at 1,640,000. Table 6 (p. 152) shows the changes in the Colony's population between 1931 and 1941.

Miss K. J. Heasman of the Department of Economics, University of Hong Kong,[2] gave the following figures for the occupation period.

1942 (rough census)   1,000,000
1944 February (estimate based on rice tickets)   850,000
1945 March (estimate based on residents'
certificates)   500,000

In May 1945 the Japanese occupation authorities counted the persons living in the Colony and obtained the figure of 650,000.

Since that time, there has been no reliable estimate of Hong Kong's population. The difficulty of estimating will be appreciated when it is realized that a figure of almost 5·7 million is given as the official sum total of arrivals in and departures from the Colony in 1950–1. Since 1953–4 the Colony's immigration authorities have virtually stopped legal entry to Hong Kong from China by introducing the policy of 'one out—one in', but illegal entry has continued.

[1] The results of the 1931 census were published in an official report written by W. J. Carrie.

[2] In a paper on *Japanese Financial and Economic Measures in Hong Kong* written in July 1945 (for private circulation only).

Both the Government of the Colony as well as various private individuals have been trying each year to estimate the size of Hong Kong's population, but discrepancies in these estimates have been very large. For example, the estimates for 1954 varied from, roughly, 2 to 3 million. Each estimate obviously produces an entirely different picture of the net migration effect, rate of natural increase, &c. and none is satisfactory. In an article published in September 1955 [1] the present author put forward an estimate which, although not pretending to be very accurate, seems to be the most consistent one from the point of view of both demographic principles and the broadly known facts about the behaviour of Hong Kong's population in the course of the first post-war decade. By applying a modified version of the so-called 'Forty Per Cent. Test' designed recently by Professor W. F. Wertheim of the University of Amsterdam [2] a solution was arrived at, the results of which are presented in Table 7 (p. 153). According to my estimate, the population of the Colony in the middle of 1954 was between 2·1 and 2·2 million and was increasing at about 3 per cent. p.a. (birth rate 39·3 per thousand, death rate 9·3 per thousand) so that in the middle of 1955 it was probably 2¼ million.[3] Thus during the decade 1945–55 the population of Hong Kong increased by about 400 per cent., if net immigration is included.

THE IMMIGRATION WAVES

The high rate of natural increase was, of course, only a comparatively minor element in Hong Kong's population pressure. A much more important factor was introduced by the migration waves. Table 8 (p. 154) shows an estimate of the net immigration into the Colony between 1945 and 1956. The series presented in this table clearly indicates two major immigration waves. The first is the wave of returning residents which came to an end some time in 1948. It would seem that already in 1946 or 1947 the population had doubled if compared with the low figure reached at the end of the Japanese occupation in the

[1] Szczepanik, 'The Hong Kong Population Puzzle', *Far East. Econ. R.*, 29 September 1955.

[2] W. F. Wertheim, 'The Forty Per Cent. Test—a Useful Demographic Tool', *Economics and Finance in Indonesia* (Djakarta), March 1955.

[3] According to a government estimate, 2,340,000 (*Hong Kong Annual Report 1955*, p. 20).

summer of 1945 (30 August). This wave was a very big one and can be estimated at approximately 700,000 persons. It had hardly ended when a new wave of refugees began to flood the Colony, reaching its peak between the middle of 1949 and the summer of 1950.[1] It would appear that this wave of refugees subsided some time in 1951–2, and after that time a period of comparative stabilization of the Colony's population began but there was again a substantial influx of immigrants from China (estimated at about 140,000) in 1955–6. The increasing prosperity of the Colony acted as a magnet.

The whole series reflects, of course, only the waves which have produced a permanent effect on the Colony's demographic structure through being absorbed by it. Temporary changes may have been much greater, but, like the tourist traffic in any country, they have not produced any lasting effect. It would be misleading, therefore, to add the figure of this highly volatile population to estimates which are to be used in demographic, economic, or sociological analysis. Thus it is possible to admit, for example, that in 1950 the population of the Colony at any given time might have been far in excess of the estimated 1·7 million, but such a number would be devoid of any analytical significance. The total size of the immigration wave of refugees can be estimated, on the basis of the series presented in Table 8, at about 500,000 persons. They have become an integral part of the Colony's population, have married, and have children born in Hong Kong. As a result of this process, their children born in the Colony and their Hong Kong-born wives have become members of 'refugee' families, automatically increasing the extent of the Colony's refugee problem.[2]

THE REFUGEE PROBLEM

It appears from the preceding discussion that the post-war acceleration in the rate of population growth in Hong Kong was chiefly caused by the influx of refugees from China as a result of

[1] From May 1950 controlled immigration of all Chinese persons was introduced and prior permission to enter the Colony was required. Commissioner of Police, *Annual Departmental Report, 1949–50*, p. 34.

[2] It should be pointed out that the estimate of the total number of refugees should take into account refugees *sur place*, i.e. those immigrants who came to the Colony before 1949 but could not return because of the political changes on the mainland.

the Communist victory. On the basis of the investigation carried out by the Hambro Mission,[1] the number of Chinese political refugees living in Hong Kong in the summer of 1954 was estimated to be 385,000 or, with their dependants, around 670,000. These figures included 285,000 refugees who fled from China for political reasons (with their dependants, 473,000 persons) and 100,000 refugees *sur place*, but did not include economic migrants, the number of which can be placed at about 400,000.

The conditions under which the refugees were living were found to be deplorable, and on the whole much worse than those of other post-war immigrants in Hong Kong. The Mission appreciated that it was out of the question for the administration to discriminate in favour of political refugees as distinct from the rest of the population, for, from the official standpoint, the refugees were merely Chinese persons living in a British Colony, and therefore could not be given special treatment. From the international point of view, however, the Mission said, they were political refugees and as such should be helped; the United Kingdom Government could not be expected to shoulder the burden alone.

Taking that principle as a starting-point, the Mission considered three conceivable solutions: repatriation, emigration, and resettlement. The first was obviously out of the question. Great difficulties had arisen over emigration, but there had been a proposal that some of the Chinese refugees should emigrate to Taiwan and elsewhere, and possibilities in that direction, however limited, were recommended for exploration.

In view of the difficulties connected with emigration and of the preference expressed by approximately one-half of the refugees, considerable attention had to be given to the firm establishment in Hong Kong of those refugees who were not yet settled, or not settled in satisfactory conditions. Here the situation was quite different from that in other countries with a refugee problem, because the Chinese refugees were treated as members of the indigenous population and their economic

[1] *The Problem of Chinese Refugees in Hongkong; Report submitted to the United Nations High Commissioner for Refugees by Dr. Edvard Hambro* (Leyden, Sijthoff, 1955) [henceforth referred to as *Hambro Report*]. The present writer acted as consultant to the Mission.

difficulties were fundamentally the same as those of the rest of the population. This made it natural and necessary to recommend steps to improve the economic position of the entire population of the Colony through construction of houses, resettlement in agriculture, and, above all, further industrial expansion. The main proposal specifically concerning the refugees was that funds should be raised with a view to helping refugees by loans or grants for vocational training, scholarships,&c. The figure put forward was HK$55 million (about US$10 million).

The UNREF Executive Committee considered the Hambro Report in May 1955 in Geneva and unanimously passed the following resolution.

The UNREF Executive Committee

Having considered the report made to the High Commissioner by Dr. E. Hambro on the problem of Chinese refugees in Hong Kong,

. . . . .

Recognizing the continuing need to alleviate the suffering of the refugees to which reference is made in the report,
Moved by its concern for the humanitarian problem involved,

1. *Notes with appreciation* the thoroughness with which the report has been drawn up;

2. *Requests* the High Commissioner:

(*a*) To give sympathetic encouragement to Governments and organizations with a view to their assisting in alleviating the problems of the Chinese refugees in Hong Kong;

(*b*) To report to the Committee, when he deems it necessary, any progress made in the implementation of this resolution.[1]

This resolution meant, in fact, that the refugees in Hong Kong are not the concern of the United Nations. Responsibility for their future was turned back to individual 'Governments and organizations', i.e. primarily to the Hong Kong Government and numerous social organizations in the Colony which have been dealing with this problem ever since it emerged.

In the absence of international financial help, and in view of emigration difficulties, Hong Kong had to rely almost entirely

---

[1] *Report of the UNREF Executive Committee (first session—Geneva, 9 to 14 May 1955)* (*General Assembly Official Records*, 10th sess., Suppl. no. 11, p. 37).

on absorption as the method of solving its refugee problem. The economic structure of the Colony proved to be flexible enough to respond to this exceptionally heavy pressure, which became one of the most important historical factors in Hong Kong's industrial revolution.

POPULATION STRUCTURE

There are certain important aspects of the post-war population structure which should be stressed here in order to understand fully the role of the human element in Hong Kong's industrial revolution.

1. First, in spite of the influx of refugees, the population remained highly homogeneous from the racial point of view. More than 99 per cent. of the population is Chinese, the great majority of whom came originally from Kwangtung Province. According to the findings of the Hambro Mission, in 1954 about 75 per cent. of the population regarded Kwangtung as their native province.[1] To this should be added 9·2 per cent. of those for whom Hong Kong became the 'native place'. An additional 6 per cent. of the population came from other provinces of South China (Fukien, Kiangsi, Hunan, Kweichow, Yunnan, and Kwangsi). Thus only about 10 per cent. of the Chinese population came from the North of China, mainly from Shanghai.

2. There was a large preponderance of men over women. In 1954 the Hambro Mission defined the ratio of men to women as 54·04 to 45·96. Connected with this was the comparatively small size of the average family, viz. 3·85, and a large percentage of working-age population, viz. 57·4 per cent., as the following figures indicate.[2]

Age	Percentage of the total population	Sex ratio
0–4	14·9	112
5–14	24·3	121
15–21	9·3	112
22–44	38·1	102
45–60	10·0	153
61–over	3·4	68

[1] *Hambro Report*, Table xiii (Statistical Appendix).
[2] Szczepanik in *Far East. Econ. R.*, 29 September 1955; *Hambro Report*.

3. The occupational structure of the immigrant population was fairly well-balanced and adjustable, as appears from Table 9 (p. 155). The large percentage of army and police, professionals and intellectuals, presented, of course, the most difficult problem in the process of industrial absorption. This explains why in 1954 about 15 per cent. of the immigrants were still without employment. The rest have become industrial labourers, coolies, domestic servants, cottage craftsmen, hawkers, &c. If related to the entire population of the Colony, the proportion of unemployed in 1954 can be estimated at about 12 per cent. of the working-age population (7 per cent. of the total population).[1] This figure clearly indicates both the speed and the difficulty of absorption of the huge influx of immigrants. No further estimates of unemployment in Hong Kong are available, but, as we shall see in the course of this study, there is reason to believe that by 1956 the percentage of unemployed, thanks to industrial progress, had substantially diminished.

[1] Table 17, p. 161.

4

The Bottleneck of Primary Industries

THE scarcity and hilly nature of the land in Hong Kong have prevented the expansion of agriculture to any significant extent. Moreover, capital has been reluctant to finance the extension of the infrastructure of local agriculture because of the legal position of the New Territories and an obsolete system of land tenure. The Colony's agriculture therefore provided but little relief to the post-war population pressure. This was an important institutional element which stimulated the growth of the manufacturing industry. Some efforts have, however, been made to improve the use of the available land, mainly by encouraging the growing of vegetables, pig breeding, and poultry farming.

In 1954-5 the total output of 23,000 acres under rice amounted to 26,000 tons of paddy or 17,600 tons of milled rice valued at approximately HK$17.6 million. Thus the value of rice output per acre was about HK$740 p.a. It was estimated that the local annual rice output only produced 8 per cent. of total demand, one month's supply.

On about 2,250 acres, approximately 62,000 tons of vegetables were grown, and their value in 1954-5 was estimated at HK$18.2 million, giving an annual value of output per acre equal to HK$8,000. In 1954-5 home-grown vegetables supplied about 45 per cent. of the Colony's consumption.[1]

On 3,500 acres, field crops such as water chestnuts, turnips,

---

[1] The following index numbers illustrate the rising trend in the production of vegetables in 1947-56 (1947-8 = 100).

1947-8	1948-9	1949-50	1950-1	1951-2	1952-3	1953-4	1954-5	1955-6
100	108	144	172	198	231	241	285	300

Source: Registrar of Co-operative Societies and Director of Marketing, *Annual Departmental Report 1955-6*, p. 21.

ginger, and lychees have been cultivated for many years; and approximately 950 acres were under orchards in 1954–5. The output of field crops (2,597 tons) was estimated at about HK$3 million, and a sum of approximately HK$1·3 million was derived from export sales. The annual value of fruit production was estimated at HK$5 million, giving a value of output per acre equal to HK$5,263.

Thus the total value of agricultural output by 1955 reached only about HK$43 million p.a., which would have been a very small share of the national income accruing to the estimated 200,000 persons living in the Colony's villages, mainly in the New Territories, had it not been supplemented by animal husbandry. Thanks to the efforts to expand pig breeding [1] and poultry farming, the total value of animal production in 1954–5 reached over HK$27 million.[2]

The value of the annual product of the agricultural sector of Hong Kong can thus be estimated at about HK$70 million. This would give only about HK$350 per person p.a. or less than one dollar a day. The situation appears even worse when it is considered that the Colony's orchards are highly commercialized and the bulk of dairying is in the hands of one large concern in Hong Kong (the Dairy Farm, Ice, & Cold Storage Co.) and one smaller enterprise in Kowloon.

According to the government estimate,[3] the annual value of output per acre was HK$875 if farming was combined with animal husbandry, and only HK$581 for farms without livestock. The average size of a family holding was estimated to be 2 acres, which would give HK$1,750 for mixed farms and HK$1,162 for farms without livestock. Assuming the average size of a farming family as equal to 4 persons, this would give only HK$438 per person p.a. for mixed farms; for farms without livestock the average annual income per person would fall to HK$290.

Furthermore, it should be noted that about 80 per cent. of the

[1] In 1955 local pig breeding supplied about 12 per cent. of the demand for pork in the Colony.

[2] It was composed as follows: pigs HK$12·0 million, dairying HK$7·4 million; poultry HK$6·0 million; ducks HK$1·5 million (export only); cattle HK$0·5 million.

[3] W. J. Blackie, *Report on Agriculture in Hong Kong with Policy Recommendations* (Hong Kong Government, 1955), p. 24.

Colony's agriculture is based on the share-tenancy system, and the landlord's share usually ranges between 40 and 60 per cent. of the crop.[1] This system seems to depress the level of farmers' income to a bare minimum of existence, making agriculture one of the least attractive occupations. So far, no efforts have been made to change the share-tenancy system in Hong Kong's agriculture, and no proposals concerning even a mild land reform have been put forward.[2] The chief difficulty consists, of course, in the fact that most of the Colony's agricultural land does not actually belong to the Crown, but is leased from China.

The low level of agricultural income and the existing share-tenancy system explain the fact that out of the 40,000 acres of cultivable land only 32,000 are in use. There is therefore still some scope for the expansion of the Colony's agricultural sector, but the capital outlay necessary for the building of new roads, irrigation, &c. has not, so far, been regarded as justifiable.

AIDS TO AGRICULTURE

The main device used to help agriculture is the vegetable-marketing scheme introduced by the Military Administration in September 1946. Under this scheme, the wholesale marketing of vegetables on the mainland is controlled and all vegetables produced in, or imported into, that area are sold wholesale in the government-organized market in Kowloon. The main aim of the scheme is the provision of transport and marketing facilities to ensure that farmers receive a fair return for their produce and are thus encouraged to grow more vegetables. Grants and loans from the Colonial Development and Welfare Fund (total HK$854,000 by the end of 1954–5) have been used to purchase a fleet of thirty-one lorries and to help in the establishment and running of the collecting centres. In 1953 the Vegetable Marketing Organization set up a revolving fund for the purpose of extending credit facilities to vegetable farmers. The loans are for productive purposes only and are made available through co-operative societies.

[1] Landlords obtain Crown land from the Government on seventy-five years' lease, but the vast majority of leases date from before 1898 and there is only a very small amount of agricultural land which can be leased.

[2] The present writer pointed this out in an article published in the *Far East. Econ. R.*, 28 February 1957.

Steady progress is being made towards the ultimate goal of making the organization fully co-operative. In March 1955 there were 15 Vegetable Marketing Societies with 3,005 members. These societies were handling nearly 60 per cent. of all locally produced vegetables marketed through the VMO. As the co-operatives take over much of the work of the organization, 3 per cent. of the 10 per cent. commission charged by the VMO. is now refunded to them. In 1953 they joined together in a Federation with the object of taking over those activities which are common to all societies and which could profitably be undertaken collectively. It is hoped that in time this Federation will take over the manifold functions of the organization.

No marketing scheme has been introduced to assist the poultry breeders and pig keepers, who are thus still at the mercy of the dealers in livestock. Some aid to these farmers, developed as help to refugees, has been provided by the Kadoorie Agricultural Aid Association.[1] When the great influx of refugees from China came to Hong Kong, many were unsuited for any occupation but farming. To help them make a start, and to increase the supply of pork in the Colony, the Kadoorie brothers, two wealthy local business men, decided to erect and stock piggeries and supply vaccines as a philanthropic activity. Breeding sows have been distributed and farmers have been assisted by gifts or interest-free loans. Breeding accommodation has been provided in up-to-date sties and sufficient feed to last nine months has been supplied to each family with two sows. The proceeds from the sale of the progeny of these sows pay off the feed loan and a small percentage of the cost of erecting the sties. Assistance has also been provided to poultrymen, in the form of free gifts of poultry, and to rice and vegetable growers, for whom some land has been opened by terracing, and irrigation systems have been installed. Interest-free loans have also enabled the farmers to buy fertilizers and the pond-fish raisers to re-stock ponds with fish fry.

The Kadoorie scheme commenced on 28 September 1951 and up to the end of May 1954 the total aid disbursed was HK$1 million. During 1954–5 the Association extended its activity

[1] *Reports of the Kadoorie Agricultural Aid Association* of 31 May 1954 and 31 December 1955.

D

towards improving irrigation and domestic water supplies; contributing to the building of access roads, paths, and drainage and protective works; diversifying agriculture by the introduction of new crops such as pineapples; and planting village orchards.

In 1955 a new venture was started, the Kadoorie Agricultural Aid (Loan) Fund. It operates a fund of half a million dollars, towards which both the Government and the Association have made equal financial contributions, while the Government has provided administrative assistance. The Fund is used to grant interest-free loans to farmers for all purposes.

Another fund which is used for financial assistance to farmers is the J. E. Joseph (Loan) Fund, set up in 1954 and amounting to HK$450,000; it is also administered by the Government and loans are granted from it at 3 per cent. p.a. Both funds together, therefore, do not reach HK$1 million, which, of course, is a very small sum. To obtain loans from traditional sources the farmer has to pay high interest charges. An interest rate of 3 per cent. or more per month is not uncommon, so that farmers become heavily indebted and their land mortgaged. As a result, they become apathetic, and descend to a very low subsistence level. The bulk of the Colony's farming population still suffers, unfortunately, from these depressing circumstances.

The Department of Agriculture, Fisheries, and Forestry, founded in 1950, aids the local farmers through its policy of protecting and developing plant and animal resources. It gives technical advice and assistance by teaching and demonstrating farming methods, encouraging the conservation of soil and water supplies, &c. The activities of the Department are co-ordinated with the Rural Development Committee. The Department's plans [1] envisage the improvement of irrigation and communications throughout the New Territories, settlement on undeveloped land, the diversification of farming to include the extension of animal industries, a soil survey, and experimental work on the introduction of new crops, the improvement of existing crop varieties, soil fertility, and the control of pests and diseases of crops and animals. Expansion of the co-operative movement among farmers is also planned.

Apart from the pressing need for land reform and the pro-

[1] Blackie, *Agriculture in Hong Kong*, pp. 69–70.

vision of more ample sources of credit and insurance facilities, insufficient attention still seems to be given to the cultivation of marginal lands, and the supply of better educational services and medical facilities for the farming population. Unless all this is done as a part of an ambitious agricultural policy, this sector of the economy will persist as one of the most awkward bottlenecks.

FISHERIES

The possibilities of expanding fisheries were early appreciated and substantial progress has been made in this sector of the economy during the post-war period, so that the achievements, particularly in the field of boat mechanization and fish marketing, were pointed out by FAO as a model to be followed in other countries of Asia and the Far East.[1]

For generations past, the *Laan* or middleman system kept the fishermen poor and in debt. A form of co-operative enterprise in which the fishermen would operate their own wholesale markets was possibly the ideal solution in this situation, but, in competition with the powerful middleman system, was scarcely likely to succeed.[2] The Government therefore decided, in October 1945, to set up an organization to control the transport and wholesale marketing of marine fish, which ensures that fishermen receive fair returns for their catch. This in turn encourages them to try out new gear and better methods of fishing, and makes possible a general improvement in their living conditions.

The Fish Marketing Organization is similar to the Vegetable Marketing Organization and maintains itself out of a 6 per cent. commission charged on all sales. It controls four wholesale fish markets where fish is sold by public auction. As fishermen operate from various scattered ports, eight collecting centres have been set up in the main fishing areas; from these centres the organization provides land or sea transport to convey the

---

[1] Szczepanik, *A Survey of Fish Marketing in the Indo-Pacific Region* (Rome, 1955), FAO Report no. 404, Part II.

[2] So far, government efforts to encourage co-operatives among the fishermen have not been very successful. By 1955 there were 20 Fishermen's Thrift and Loan Societies, but their total membership was only 389. On the whole, great difficulty is experienced with fishermen's societies, in which it is often difficult to find members who are sufficiently literate to keep the simplest accounts.

catch to the markets. Assistance is also given by the staff of these centres in obtaining licences for boats, registering personnel, settling disputes, securing medical treatment, and so forth. Through the organization's supply section, ice, fish hooks, drinking-water, diesel oil, lubricating oil, &c. are sold to the fishermen at the lowest possible prices. Until December 1954 rationed rice was also sold, but when rationing of rice was abolished, it was decided to suspend its supplies. As part of the welfare programme of the FMO, in 1955 over 1,350 fishermen's children were receiving education at schools wholly or partially financed by the organization.

Between 1945 and 1955 there has been steady progress in the mechanization of the fishing industry in Hong Kong. By the end of 1955 there were 890 mechanized boats, whereas in 1945 all fishing craft were wind-driven. Much of the mechanization has been facilitated by credit provided by local engineering companies. At the request of interested fishermen, the FMO deducted money from proceeds of sales of fish in order to pay off these loans. Similar facilities have been afforded to those fishermen who borrowed money from the Junk Mechanization Loan Fund operated by the Department of Agriculture, Fisheries, and Forestry and financed by the Colonial Development and Welfare Fund. In September 1946 a loan of HK$250,000 was received from the Government for the purpose of establishing a revolving fund to issue loans to fishermen at low interest for productive purposes. This loan was completely repaid in 1949, and the organization now operates its own revolving fund.

The Colony's fishing fleet now consists of over 6,000 junks, 15 per cent. of which are mechanized, and 31 Japanese-type trawlers. They are manned by a sea-fishing population of 56,000 [1] or by approximately 14,000 fishing families. The total quantity of fish landed in 1954–5 was about 40,000 tons. This would give an average annual output of 3 tons per fishing family, without counting subsistence fishing. The total value of the output of Hong Kong's fishing industry in 1954–5 amounted to HK$45·2 million,[2] which would give HK$3,000 p.a. per fishing family or approximately HK$750 per person

---

[1] In 1945 the fishing population of the Colony was estimated at 26,257 persons.
[2] Fresh fish HK$34·6 million, salt/dried fish HK$4·8 million, pond fish HK$1·0 million, oyster culture HK$4·6 million, shrimps and fish fry HK$0·2 million.

per year. This income was roughly the same as in the manufacturing industry and almost twice as high as in agriculture.

The increase in the output of fish has been accompanied by a marked downward trend of prices, although fluctuations resulting from the instability of demand and supply were also visible. Table 10 (p. 156) illustrates these trends of supply and prices.

Although Hong Kong still imports most of the fresh-water fish consumed, the supply of marine fish is now evidently meeting the demand, and it would appear that the next step required is to develop overseas markets for the Colony's marine-fish surplus, presumably in some processed form. Unfortunately, the commercial export of salt/dried fish was seriously affected when the Chinese authorities banned its import into China in 1950. This ban is still in force, but new markets are being established in Singapore, Indonesia, the Philippines, Canada, and the United States. Apart from the export of salt/dried fish and fish fry, exportable commodities are now provided by oyster culture in the New Territories.

There are many good reasons to believe that there is considerable scope for further expansion of the Colony's fishing industry and of allied industries, such as fish processing, canning, &c., which could provide employment for a great number of people and generate a substantial income.[1]

FORESTRY

So far, forestry in Hong Kong can hardly be regarded as an income-generating sector. In 1954–5 the total value of local trees sold did not exceed HK$100,000. Consequently, the Colony's building, paper, and plastic industries have had to rely exclusively on imported timber. During the Japanese occupation most of the Colony's forests were destroyed. An afforestation plan was not designed until 1953,[2] when 3,000 acres were set aside as the initial plantation area, of which

---

[1] For fuller discussion of these possibilities, see Szczepanik, 'An Introduction to the Economic Analysis of Fishery in the Far East', *Economics and Finance in Indonesia*, July 1956.

In December 1956 the present writer carried out a survey of Hong Kong's fishing industry as part of a regional research project sponsored by FAO. The results of this survey are being prepared for publication.

[2] A. F. Robertson, *A Review of Forestry in Hong Kong* (Hong Kong Government, 1953), pp. 3–4, 29–30.

about 1,000 acres are now planted with trees every year. For this purpose, the production of 1 million plants a year has been organized at the Tai Lung Nursery (near Fan Ling in the New Territories). At the same time, efforts are being made to interest villagers in the government scheme of assistance for the planting of village forestry lots, and to extend amenity planting throughout the New Territories.

In 1954 a new large-scale forest project was undertaken by a private enterprise, the Lantao Development Co.[1] Its main plan consists in the afforestation of an initial area of 5,000 acres on Lantao (a fairly large and comparatively undeveloped island) with the Hoop Pine (a rough-barked soft-wood tree). The first crop of firewood and scrap for pulping is expected in the fifth year after planting. Timber felling should take place in the tenth year. Planting goes on at the rate of about 1·5 million saplings a year (i.e. more than the output of the main government nursery at Fan Ling), and it is planned to cover the whole area in ten years. Harvesting of up to 1 million trees a year should be more or less continuous from that time. The increasing use of soft-wood pulp for paper, plastics, and the manufacture of building boards should make this a readily marketable commodity and possibly the basis for a string of other local industries. The project, however, does not need to wait ten years for its first financial return. The first major income of the Company was expected in 1957 from the sale of pond fish. Plans are also made for a 20,000-acre cattle-rearing project.

In making plans to develop Lantao, the Company revived the ideas of some early founders of the Colony who wanted to settle there because there was more flat land available for rural development. The argument that won the battle for Hong Kong was that the contours and streams on that island were better suited for water conservancy. It is likely that the formation of the Lantao Development Co. will mark a new phase in the economic history of the Colony.

QUARRYING AND MINING

The exploitation of local quarries and sand deposits has contributed greatly to the post-war development of the building

[1] W. J. Smyly, 'Lantao Development—Soft Wood in Hong Kong', *Hongkong Exporter and Far Eastern Importer*, 1956–7.

and construction industry. Quarrying, crushing, and screening of Hong Kong granite is carried out in plants all over the Colony operated by the Roads Office of the Public Works Department. All grades and types of stones are shaped and curved, the ornamental grey granite being most commonly worked for building stone. Between 1952 and 1955 the output of building stone has more than doubled, increasing from 92,000 to 209,000 tons. Another important item of the government quarries is the production of road metal. This output has also been steadily increasing, and reached 56,000 tons in 1955. Some road metal and even dressed stone have been exported to Borneo. The value of the total output of government quarries is estimated at about HK$3 million p.a.

On most of the beaches around the Colony there are deposits of sand which is used for building, foundries, and glass making. Since 1935 the exploitation of these deposits has been under the control of the Government Sand Monopoly, the main object of which is to preserve the beaches. In 1949–50 about 355,000 cubic yards of sand were removed and transported throughout the Colony, which provided about HK$3 million gross of income to the Government. In 1955–6 the sales of sand increased to 570,000 cubic yards and the Government's gross income to HK$4·9 million. The expenses of collection, storage, and distribution left only a small net profit.

Until the Second World War mining in Hong Kong never possessed any substantial economic significance.[1] Some minerals, such as lead, iron ore, wolfram (tungsten), tin, and even occasionally gold and silver, were mined for a fairly long period but on a very limited scale. After the war, the most important factor contributing to a more intensive exploitation of the Colony's mineral wealth was the decline in trade relations with China. Supplies of tin, antimony, and wolfram from South and West China were cut off. Thus new efforts arose in Hong Kong to look for these minerals, especially wolfram and iron ore.

Lead was the first metallic mineral to be mined in Hong Kong since the middle of the nineteenth century, near Silver Mine Bay (on Lantao Island) and near Li Ma Hang (along the

[1] S. G. Davis, *The Geology of Hong Kong* (Hong Kong, Government Printer, 1952), pp. 109–23.

Shum Chun river). Li Ma Hang proved to possess the largest deposit of lead, and this mine was worked fairly regularly from the First World War until 1940, annual output exceeding 3,000 tons. But the Japanese, when withdrawing in 1945, removed most of the equipment and no further substantial investment in lead mines has been made. Since the Second World War output has not exceeded 750 tons p.a. It is destined mainly for export to the United Kingdom and Europe. In 1955 the value of lead output was HK$327,000.

Hydrated iron deposits (limonite) have been used as fillers in paint production since the end of the nineteenth century. In 1906 a fairly large deposit of magnetite was opened at Ma On Shan (on the north-eastern ridge of Kowloon peninsula) with an estimated reserve of 8–9 million tons. Exploitation of this mine before the Second World War was regulated by its chief customer, the Green Island Cement Co. After the war the development of the mine was stimulated by the Japanese demand, which raised the output from 908 tons in 1948 to 115,500 tons in 1955. In 1953 an agreement was reached with a Japanese firm to instal an electro-magnetic dressing plant at the cost of HK$2·5 million, and to convert the mine from open-cast to underground working. This installation and conversion were completed in 1956 and the mine is expected to produce up to 300,000 tons p.a. The value of the magnetite mined for export (mainly to Japan) amounted in 1955 to HK$3·5 million, and for local use to about HK$1 million. Besides this, some surface scratchings for ochre, a hydrated oxide of iron, are undertaken. The ochre is used as raw material by several local paint factories.

Exploitation of the local deposits of wolfram began in 1917, when the value of wolfram for hardening steel was discovered. The Japanese kept up a steady production of wolfram during their occupation, and this production continued after the war. As all the wolfram was destined for export, mainly to the United Kingdom and France, its output varied according to the world market price. In 1952 the annual output was estimated to be as high as 900 tons and its value exceeded HK$2½ million. Two years later the price fell so low that exploitation by surface scratching by amateurs was almost abandoned. In 1955 only 23 tons of wolfram (valued at about HK$150,000) were produced. The main deposits, exploited by a European-owned concern, are at Shing Mun, in Castle Peak area, and minor deposits are found at Ho Chung, and Sha Lo Wan on Lantao Island.

Intensification of geological research in Hong Kong in recent years resulted in the discovery of graphite in 1953 on West Brother Island off Castle Peak, and of beryl in 1955. The natural amorphous graphite shows a fixed carbon content of 80–87 per cent., and over 1,500 tons of it have already been exported to the United Kingdom, the United States, and Japan in 1954 and 1955. It is expected that about 2,000 tons of graphite may be exported each year, which would amount to almost 1 per cent. of the world output of this rare mineral, now in high demand in connexion with nuclear industry. Two new areas in the New Territories thought to contain graphite deposits are being prospected.[1]

Beryl was discovered in two areas, one of which is being prospected in order to ascertain whether the ore can be worked on a commercial basis. According to provisional estimates, there is a reserve of about 500 tons of this mineral.[2]

One fortunate result of the weathering process is the production of various types of clays. The total annual output of clays fluctuates between 5,000 and 6,000 tons (about HK$350,000). Of the many deposits now being worked, the pit at Cha Kwo Ling is the most valuable and productive. Much of the clay from this pit is exported to Japan, but some is used locally in the ceramic industry. It is used for high-grade pottery and as a filler for paper, rubber, and cloth. Elsewhere other deposits are mined for the various brick, face-powder, tooth-powder, and rubber companies. In the New Territories there are many brick factories located on or near the clay deposits. The two largest ceramic factories at San Hui (Castle Peak) are producing not only bricks but also high-grade pipe-ware and tiles.

Apart from clays, economic deposits of felspar (a crystalline white or flesh-red mineral) occur in all parts of the Colony in association with the granite masses. They are mined for use in glaze and enamelware in local factories.

The total value of the output of minerals in Hong Kong in

[1] B. Ruxton, 'Graphite in Hong Kong', *Far East. Econ. R.*, 27 January 1955.
[2] idem, 'The Occurrence of Beryl in Hong Kong', ibid. 12 May 1955.

1955 was estimated at HK$6 million, to which should be added the value of the output of quarries (about HK$3 million) and the income of the Sand Monopoly (about HK$5 million), giving the total value of mining output as equal to approximately HK$14 million. Total employment in this group of primary industries amounts to about 2,000 persons, but it is very irregular.

At present, mining policy in the Colony is formulated by the Mines Department, which remains under the general control of the Commissioner of Labour. In 1954 the Mining Bill, including the Mining (General) Regulations and the Mining (Safety) Regulations, was passed. Under these Regulations, the Government issues prospecting licences for 6 months (renewable every 6 months up to 2 years), mining licences for 6 months (renewable up to 5 years), and mining leases up to 21 years (renewable at the discretion of the Governor-in-Council). Apart from fixing the licence fees, rents, and premiums, the Regulations determine the royalties at 5 per cent. of the value of all minerals won, based on the local price or f.o.b. price.

In order to ensure proper exploitation, the Regulations stipulate that the expenditure by the holder of a prospecting licence shall be at the rate of not less than HK$10 per acre each month, and that the holder of a mining licence or mining lease shall continuously employ at least 5 persons for every 10 acres. Labour-saving apparatus calculated at the rate of 1 h.p. to 5 persons may be accepted in substitution for the number of persons specified above.

This new legal framework, combined with the intensification of geological research, may contribute towards increasing the economic importance of mining in Hong Kong, but no optimistic expectations can be attached to it, in the same way as no great prospects lie before the Colony's agriculture.

5

Decline in the Traditional Source of Income

POST-WAR CHANGES IN HONG KONG'S TRADE

EVER since the foundation of the Colony, entrepôt trade has been the traditional source of its income. During the post-war period both the volume and value as well as the direction of Hong Kong's entrepôt trade have undergone considerable changes, which, together with population pressure, formed the second outstanding historical factor in Hong Kong's industrial revolution.

Before we embark on the analysis of these changes it is necessary to have a clear quantitative picture. Table 11 (p. 156) shows the value of the Colony's foreign trade between 1946 and 1956. In order to facilitate comparison, the trade value data have been converted into index numbers with 1948 taken as a basis. Graph I illustrates this table. These statistics indicate that during the reconstruction period of 1946–8 the value of Hong Kong's exports and imports doubled. In 1948, the first post-war year of relative political and economic stability in the Colony, the import surplus amounted to about HK$500 million. During the next three years the value of the Colony's trade increased by another 150 per cent. The value of exports increased faster than that of imports, so that the deficit in the balance of trade was almost eliminated in 1950, the year when the value index of exports rose from 146 to 235 in one year. Then the 'Korean boom' of 1950–1 followed, but it was a short-lived phenomenon. In 1952 the value index of total trade declined to 182 from 254 in 1951; it dropped further in 1953 and 1954, when the total value of trade reached its lowest point at about 60 per cent. above the 1948 level, with the deficit in the balance of trade approximately twice as large as in 1948.

This trade depression lasted for about three years. One of its most important economic consequences was the switch from

GRAPH I

Indices of Post-war Foreign Trade

(*1948 = 100*)

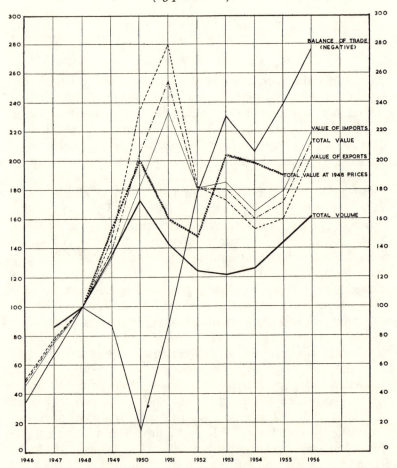

Source: Tables 11, 12 and 13, Statistical Appendix.

entrepôt trade to manufacturing industries, which became the new main source of the Colony's income. In 1955 occurred the first visible improvement in the value of the Colony's trade by about 7 per cent. over the preceding year. However, as the value of imports rose somewhat faster, the import surplus became larger, reaching the level of about HK$1,200 million.

Changes in the quantum of trade are shown in Table 12 (p. 157) and also in Graph I. Comparison of the behaviour of the value and volume index numbers during the post-war period indicates that the volume index fluctuated much less widely than the value index. The former rose only 73 per cent. above the 1948 level, the latter 154 per cent. Similarly, the decline of volume during the depression period was not as violent as the decrease in value.[1] Another interesting point is that the post-war volume peak was reached in 1950, whereas the value peak occurred a year later, in 1951. Contrasted with this, the lowest point of the volume level occurred in 1953, a year before the value minimum, reached in 1954. Finally, the substantial rise in the volume index from 126 in 1954 to 144 in 1955 proves that in 1955 there was a marked revival in the Colony's entrepôt trade. Whereas the total value increased by 7 per cent., the volume rose by 14 per cent. above the 1954 level. As a result, the volume of Hong Kong's trade in 1955 was almost identical with the 1951 boom volume, although still below the 1950 volume peak.

An analysis of the changes in foreign trade should take into account the changes in the purchasing power of money. In the period of changing prices the picture of unadjusted current values is misleading. On the other hand, the volume analysis does not contain enough data. The solution is normally found by converting the current value data into figures adjusted for price changes. For our purpose, it is convenient to take 1948 prices as a basis. In Table 13 (p. 157), a specially constructed index of wholesale prices is employed, in the absence of a suitable official price index. It will be noticed that our wholesale price index is not very satisfactory because of the small number of commodities on which it is constructed and because of the constancy of the weights used. In spite of this, it fairly

[1] One reason for this phenomenon was the great variation of profit margins at the time.

well reflects the trend of prices between 1948 and 1955. When it is applied to the data on the total trade value, the following points clearly emerge.

In real value (or 'wealth') terms, the post-war peak in Hong Kong's trade was reached in 1950, at a level almost twice as high as in 1948. In 1951 the Colony experienced an apparent boom, which was purely inflationary, and was, in real terms, a decline. This decline continued in 1952, when the bottom of depression was reached at 47 per cent. above the 1948 level. In 1953, however, there was already some recovery in the flow of wealth through Hong Kong. In 1955, in real terms, the Colony's trade stood at approximately 90 per cent. above the 1948 level, i.e. about 10 per cent. below the 1950 peak. This picture therefore is not as rosy as the unadjusted value or volume figures seem to indicate, but it proves that in 1955 there was a real tendency towards improvement.

The significance of the increasing deficit in the balance of trade in the Colony will be analysed in the concluding chapter of this book. Generally speaking, the excess of imports over exports is an indication of the speed with which Hong Kong was industrialized and a symptom of the growing value of the Colony's national income. This import surplus was offset by capital movements and the 'invisible' earnings accruing through shipping, insurance companies, &c., and through the increasing volume of tourist expenditure.

THE EFFECTS OF THE EMBARGO

The decline in the value of Hong Kong's external trade between 1951 and 1952 produced a violent shock to the whole economy. Assuming that the gross rate of profits in the entrepôt trade amounted to 17 per cent. of the value of exports,[1] earnings from this traditional source of income fell from HK$644 million to HK$421 million, i.e. by about 35 per cent., which was aggravated by the decline in the earnings of warehouses, transport, banking, insurance companies, &c. This heavy decline might have produced a reduction of the Colony's national income by about one-third; this actually did not occur, thanks to a rapid switch towards manufacturing industries.

[1] Szczepanik, 'The Gains of Entrepôt Trade', *Far East. Econ. R.*, 16 December 1954.

The cause of this violent decline in the value of Hong Kong's entrepôt trade can be attributed to the Communist occupation of the mainland and, connected with it, to the imposition on 18 May 1951 of the United Nations embargo on the export of strategic commodities to China, which has been rigidly enforced by the Hong Kong Government. The resolution was the direct result of China's participation in the Korean War. The imposition of this embargo was followed not only by a very sharp fall in Hong Kong's exports to China, but also by a drastic reduction of the total value of Hong Kong's trade.

Table 14 (p. 158) indicates that in 1955 the value of Hong Kong's exports to China constituted only 7·2 per cent. of the total value of the Colony's exports. As an importing country, China shifted to fifth place, with only HK$182 million in 1955, whereas the imports of Malaya amounted to HK$375 million, the United Kingdom HK$252 million, Indonesia HK$193 million, and South Korea HK$192 million. This should be compared with the situation in 1951, when China's imports from Hong Kong constituted 36·2 per cent. of the Colony's total exports and thus gave China first importance as trading partner. Throughout this whole period, 1951–5, Hong Kong's imports from China were remarkably stable. As a result, the Colony's balance of trade with China turned from a surplus of HK$741 million in 1951 into a deficit of HK$715 million in 1955.

However, comparison of exports to China in 1950–1 with trade after the imposition of the embargo is misleading. A better comparison seems to be with 1948, when exports to China constituted 17·7 per cent. of Hong Kong's total exports and the excess of imports from China over exports to China amounted to about HK$150 million. The period 1950–1 was completely exceptional because of China's feverish buying prior to and during the Korean War, the availability of previously frustrated stocks in Hong Kong, and the closure of Shanghai, Tientsin, &c., which forced practically all China's ocean-borne foreign trade through Hong Kong. On the other hand, it is necessary to take into account the trade which, while visible in 1950 and 1951, continued later in the form of direct shipments to Chinese ports negotiated by Hong Kong merchants. Unfortunately no figures concerning this trade are available.

The main effect of the embargo has been on the following goods: natural rubber and latex, synthetic rubber, petroleum oils and mixtures of oils, certain classes of iron and steel, transport equipment, and machinery. The value of the exports of these items from Hong Kong to China amounted to HK$470 million in 1950 (about 13 per cent. of the total value of Hong Kong exports) and HK$676 million in the first half of 1951.[1] In 1955, the fifth year of the United Nations embargo, China's imports of these items from Hong Kong amounted to only HK$3·7 million, and this sum included the deliveries to foreign diplomats in China.[2]

Since 1953, as a result of the relaxation of international tension, significant changes have been made in the British export-licensing control, but until June 1956 these changes did not apply to China, Macao, Tibet, and North Vietnam. As a result, there arose a considerable difference between the Soviet and the Chinese lists of embargoed goods, the latter being much longer. Compared to China, therefore, the USSR could import a wider variety of goods from the non-Communist countries which observed the United Nations embargo resolution. About 400 export items were barred to China, while the control list for trade with the USSR consisted of 264 items. In June 1956 the British Government took the first steps towards the relaxation of the embargo, in conformity with the opinion strongly held by business men that restrictions applicable to the trade with China should not be more severe than those on exports to the USSR and other Communist countries. A year later, in June 1957, the British embargo on the export of strategic goods to China became identical with the restrictions applicable to the USSR.

In a separate article,[3] the present writer attempted to find out how much Hong Kong's trade would be increased by the reduction of the Chinese list to the same proportions as the

[1] The total value of exports from Hong Kong to China (excluding Taiwan) in the first half of 1951 was HK$1,151 million.

[2] For detailed analysis of these changes, see E. F. Szczepanik and Ng Kwok Leung, 'The Embargo Problem', *Hongkong Exporter and Far Eastern Importer*, 1956–7.

[3] Szczepanik and Ng Kwok Leung, in *Hongkong Exporter and Far Eastern Importer*, 1956–7.

Russian. The figure arrived at was HK$1,213 million p.a. as a possible maximum. If, however, comparison is made with 1948, a realistic estimate would have to be placed at only about HK$150 million. On the other hand, assuming that China's imports from Hong Kong revert to about 17 per cent. of Hong Kong's total exports as in 1948, then the possible increase would amount to approximately HK$500 million. To conclude, the increase of China's imports from Hong Kong may fluctuate between HK$150 million and HK$500 million p.a. Doubts may arise as to China's capacity to pay for the imports in question. In 1955 (as mentioned above) China had a favourable trade balance with Hong Kong amounting to more than HK$700 million. It is very likely that Hong Kong's re-exports of Chinese goods to South East Asia will substantially increase in quantity and variety. Thus the increase of China's imports from Hong Kong could possibly be balanced by China's increasing exports to Hong Kong and by personal remittances from the overseas Chinese of sterling to China, estimated at around £50 million (HK$800 million) a year. From the Colony's point of view, such an increase in the volume of trade would be of great importance. It would amount to an increase of about 5–15 per cent. in the value of the Colony's total exports above the 1956 level. No wonder, therefore, that the matter is regarded as the foremost economic problem of Hong Kong. Various unpredictable factors, such as direct agreements with the supplying countries and unwillingness of China to import via Hong Kong, as well as other economic and political considerations, may reduce the actual value of Hong Kong's exports to China far below the above-quoted estimate. Nevertheless, the recent changes in the British embargo on the export of strategic goods to China may be the first step on the road towards normalization of economic relations between China and Hong Kong.

THE LOSS OF THE CHINESE MARKET FOR CAPITAL GOODS

Apart from the effects of the embargo, which applied to strategic commodities, trade with China was considerably reduced because of the political changes on the mainland. The Communist take-over resulted, first of all, in a drastic cut in imports of all kinds of consumer goods from abroad. More

E

interesting and important, however, was a radical change in the sources of supply of capital goods to China. The new régime secured substantial deliveries of producers' goods from the Soviet bloc which replaced the industrial countries of Europe and America as well as Japan. All these changes had a very great effect on the volume of Hong Kong's entrepôt trade with China.

In a separate article [1] the present author has analysed the changes in Hong Kong's entrepôt trade in non-strategic capital goods between 1953 and 1954, i.e. during the phase when this trade to China dwindled to the very small amount of HK$16 million (£1 million). The analysis comprised twenty-three items which together constituted the bulk of the capital goods imported and actually exported from Hong Kong during 1953 and 1954. In 1953 the total export value of these goods was HK$127·2 million. This figure, if combined with the small items not included in the analysis, gives a rough total of approximately £8 million. The total value of Hong Kong exports in 1953, less the value of locally manufactured goods, amounted to about £120 million. Thus the share of capital goods in the Colony's entrepôt trade in 1953 was about 6½ per cent. Obviously, therefore, in 1953 the importance of entrepôt trade in capital goods in Hong Kong was very small, and this decline was mainly due to the reduced volume of exports to China, which was still the main importer of these commodities through Hong Kong.

In 1954 the entrepôt trade in capital goods further deteriorated. Whereas the total level of the Colony's entrepôt trade in 1954 fell by 17 per cent. below the 1953 level, the value of entrepôt trade in capital goods declined by 56 per cent. to about HK$56 million and constituted only 3·2 per cent. of the total value of the Colony's entrepôt trade in the year 1954.

On the buyers' side, in 1953 China's demand was still by far the greatest, in spite of a heavy quantitative decline. In 1953 the export of capital goods to China amounted to HK$82 million, which represented about 65 per cent. of the total, whereas Indonesia, which came second, imported from the

[1] Szczepanik, 'Entrepôt Trade in Capital Goods in Hong Kong', *Far East. Econ. R.*, 14 July 1955.

Colony only HK$16 million, i.e. approximately 13 per cent. The other Far Eastern buyers (Indochina, the Philippines, Thailand, &c.) were of much smaller significance. In 1954 the situation deteriorated further because the figure for China dropped to HK$16 million, i.e. to 28 per cent. of the total value of Hong Kong's entrepôt trade in capital goods.

In 1953 Western Germany, Japan, and the United Kingdom were the three main suppliers. The values of capital goods imported from these countries were HK$54·5 million, HK$52·5 million, and HK$47·5 million respectively, whereas the figure for the United States, which came fourth in the list, was only HK$6·7 million. Thus the decline in China's demand has affected chiefly these four countries. In 1954 the United Kingdom and Japan still took the lead in capital goods, exporting to Hong Kong HK$31·9 million and HK$31·4 million respectively, while the value for Western Germany dropped from HK$54·5 million to only HK$9·6 million.

The decline in the importance of the Chinese market for capital goods continued in 1955, when the total value of these goods sent from Hong Kong to China fell to about HK$4 million, whereas the total value of entrepôt trade in capital goods was slightly above the 1954 level (HK$60 million). China fell to the sixth place on the list of importers, and Indochina became the largest buyer (HK$12 million), followed by Thailand, Indonesia, Malaya, and South Korea.

During 1955 the United Kingdom and Japan were still the main suppliers of capital goods to Hong Kong, but the position of other countries was greatly affected by exports from China. Already in 1954 there was a significant increase in the value of capital goods sent *from* China through Hong Kong. The value of this item increased from HK$0·3 million in 1953 to HK$2·2 million in 1954. The position of China as supplier of capital goods improved further in 1955, so that in the first half of 1956 she shifted to the third place after Japan and the United Kingdom, but before the United States and Western Germany. The variety of goods supplied by China was not very large: deliveries included mainly nails, tacks, spikes, bolts, nuts, and washers of all base metals, and sheet glass, but some sewing-machines and office machinery were also supplied.

As far as the composition of trade is concerned, the period

1955–6 was characterized by a further decline in the importance of such items as electrical and radiological apparatus, optical and medical instruments, and office machinery. Sewing-machines became the most important item of trade; these were followed by iron and steel bars, nails and tacks, textile machinery, and various small machines. The United Kingdom and Japan were the chief suppliers of sewing-machines through Hong Kong to Indochina, Korea, Malaya, and Indonesia. China was the main supplier of nails and tacks. Textile machinery came mainly from Japan and the United Kingdom, and various small machines from the United Kingdom. This development resulted not only in the re-direction of Hong Kong's entrepôt trade in capital goods, but also in a change in its composition. Following this, there was in 1956 a marked improvement in its total value. The analysis of these changes falls outside the scope of this book. We have to stress, however, in the concluding part of this section that China, from a country importing capital goods through Hong Kong, is herself becoming an exporter of these goods. This observation is of great significance as far as the prospects of Hong Kong's entrepôt trade are concerned.

THE PROSPECTS OF ENTREPÔT TRADE

The analysis carried out in this chapter has shown that the loss of the Chinese market produced a heavy decline in all lines of Hong Kong's entrepôt trade. This reduction in the traditional source of the Colony's income became a powerful stimulus to find a new source of wealth through a rapid development of manufacturing industries. We have observed also, however, that from 1955 onwards there was a marked revival in Hong Kong's entrepôt trade, so that in 1956 the Colony was hoping to expand along two lines, commercial and industrial, simultaneously. Whether these hopes will materialize is difficult to say, but the following considerations may help to outline the prospects of Hong Kong's entrepôt trade.

First, we have to bear in mind that the entrepôt trade has the character of a two-way traffic. In the past, on the one hand, Hong Kong merchants were buying in Asian markets, and selling all over the world, various raw materials (such as bristles, seeds, raw silk, animal and vegetable oils, &c.) of mainly agricultural origin, and a wide range of consumption goods (such as tea, embroideries, pottery, articles of oriental art and craft, &c.) being the products of either farming or cottage industries. On the other hand, Hong Kong imported industrial raw materials and finished producers' and consumers' goods mainly from the Western countries and Japan in order to sell them in the Far Eastern markets.

Ever since 1951, owing to reduction in demand rather than supply, the size of the first circuit has been declining. The effects of the United States embargo imposed on goods of Chinese origin have been important. But the results of the development of new methods of production, such as synthetic fibres, oils, fats, &c., cannot be overlooked. The products of Far Eastern farming and cottage industries encounter strong competition. Apart from this, artistic production does not seem to thrive in Communist China, which has always been the largest participant in the Colony's entrepôt trade.

The decline in the size of the first circuit has had considerable influence in reducing the entrepôt trade in capital goods. This fact may have been obscured by the relatively large import of capital goods necessary for the development of local industries. There are also, however, certain permanent reasons why the entrepôt trade in capital goods cannot assume important dimensions. To prove this point, it is necessary to examine the structure of the demand for these goods.

The main component parts of this demand are, first, standardized and not bulky tools, instruments, apparatus, and small machines, and secondly, bulky and specific semi-finished products and machinery, transport equipment, factory plant, &c. Hong Kong has practically no chance of regaining the entrepôt trade in the second of the above-mentioned categories. Better chances, however, exist in the first category, where the display of samples can be easily arranged and where, moreover, it pays to buy from Hong Kong wholesalers, as considerable transport economies, advantages of bulk-breaking, &c. can often be achieved. But, in general, the future of the entrepôt trade in capital goods depends mainly on such unpredictable events as political changes, natural calamities, need for rearmament or for post-war reconstruction, changes in technical methods, and the discovery of new raw materials. The success of Hong Kong merchants in the past has been due to the fact that they were always very sensitive to such changes, switching quickly from one line of business to another, often perhaps unnecessarily speculative, but constantly firm in their fight for economic survival on the barren rock which in the course of a century has been transformed into one of the busiest trading centres in the world. As long as this traditional merchant-adventurer attitude persists in the Colony, its entrepôt trade will continue, but it must be remembered that the trade in capital goods requires a great deal more specialized knowledge than the trade in consumer goods; and thus new opportunities may often be missed by Hong Kong dealers. On the other hand, there is little doubt that the future will provide such opportunities for Hong Kong middlemen specializing in capital goods. Korean reconstruction and the war in Indochina serve as the most recent examples of factors which considerably affected the trade in capital goods through Hong Kong.

The general structure of Hong Kong entrepôt trade indicates that the trade in capital goods depends on the extent of the first circuit (trade in Eastern goods sold in the West), and on the relative share of raw materials and consumers' goods in the second circuit (trade in Western goods sold in the East). Should the first circuit be small, the prospects of entrepôt trade in capital goods would be poor. On the other hand, the decline in demand for industrial raw materials and consumption goods supplied by the West may enhance the demand for capital goods in the Far East.

A change in the total structure of the demand of many Far Eastern countries is now taking place—a change against consumption goods and in favour of capital goods and industrial raw materials. It would, however, be unwise to expect too much from this change, for it should be borne in mind that it is due, especially in China, to a major social revolution which has also brought radical changes in the methods of foreign trade. Exchange controls, bilateral barter agreements, and state bulk-buying are nowadays widely accepted not only by Communist China, but also by other Far Eastern countries. This implies the policy of directly contacting the producers themselves and by-passing Hong Kong middlemen. At the moment China arranges most of her purchases of capital goods from Soviet satellites through East Berlin. It seems likely that if she decides to extend her purchases from Western countries, it will be done through some West European trading centre rather than Hong Kong. Awareness of this fact is one of the main driving forces behind Hong Kong's industrial expansion which we shall examine in the subsequent part of this book.

III
THE INDUSTRIAL REVOLUTION

6

The Nature and Mechanism of the Industrial Revolution

THE pressure of refugees from China was not able to find an outlet in the declining entrepôt trade of the Colony. Emigration on a large scale proved impossible, and the local primary industries offered little scope for the absorption of new labour. However, an opening for new employment was found in the expansion of manufacturing industries.

Graph II and Table 15 (p. 159) illustrate the increase in employment and the growth in the number of 'registered and recorded' factories and workshops during the post-war period.[1] These statistics do not include unregistered industrial establishments and domestic workers, but it seems reasonable to assume that the growth of this 'unregistrable' sector of industry proceeded at the same rate as that of the registered and recorded sector. Thus if 1948 is taken as a base, the index number of factories by 1956 increased to 253 and the index of industrial employment to 226.

Parallel with the growth in numbers were the increase in the variety of the lines of manufacture, and the resulting shift in the relative importance of various industries. In general, the 'old' industries declined and 'new' industries gained in importance. Thus in 1947 shipbuilding and ship repairing was the most important industry in the Colony as it absorbed about 28 per cent. of the labour force in the registered and recorded establish-

[1] A 'recorded' establishment is one that is not registrable under the Factories and Workshops Ordinance but is kept under observation because from fifteen to nineteen workers are employed. The installation of power-driven machinery or an increase to twenty or more in the number of persons employed would render the premises registrable. Inspections are made of such establishments and the proprietors are advised regarding industrial health and safety. Other types of recorded establishments are those in which women or young persons are employed, or in which the materials or processes in use may present health or safety hazards to workers.

GRAPH II

Number of Registered and Recorded Factories and Industrial Workers

$(1948 = 100)$

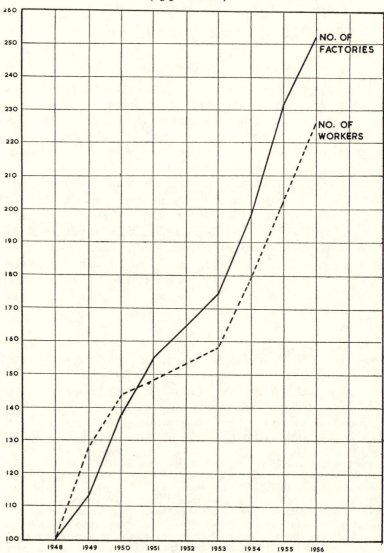

Source: Table 15, Statistical Appendix.

ments. In 1955 this top place passed to the textile industry. In the manufacture of metal products, in 1947 about 8·5 per cent. of the registered industrial labour force was employed, whereas in 1955 this figure increased to 13·3 per cent., shifting to second place after textiles. Table 16 (p. 160) illustrates in detail the employment structure in 1955, as reflected in the official statistics covering the registered and recorded establishments.

In the absence of total employment statistics, it is difficult to evaluate the growth of the relative importance of employment in manufacturing industries. The official statistics of employment in registered and recorded factories comprise more than the manufacturing industries (e.g. electricity, gas, laundries, communications, storage, warehousing, mining, recreation services). Thus the figure of 115,000 given for 1954 is somewhat higher (by about 5 per cent.) than employment in manufacturing industry alone. On the other hand, as the government estimate of 100,000 persons employed in unregistrable industrial establishments or as outworkers is probably too low, total employment in the manufacturing industry in 1954 may be taken as equal to about 230,000 persons altogether. If the total gainfully employed population in 1954 is estimated at 760,000 (see Table 17, p. 161), employment in manufacturing industry would amount to approximately 30 per cent. It appears that by 1955 about one-third of the total gainfully employed population was engaged in manufacturing industry, which thus became the main source of employment in the Colony.

The resulting large increase in manufacturing output could not, obviously, be absorbed entirely by local demand. Thus another important, 'revolutionary' feature of the post-war economic growth of Hong Kong was the increase in the volume and value of exports of locally manufactured goods. In 1947 they formed only 10 per cent of the Colony's total exports. This figure rose to 25 per cent. in 1952 and to 30 per cent. in 1953, remaining at this level throughout 1954 and 1955. Total exports of Hong Kong products in 1953 amounted to about £40 million, in 1954 to £42 million, and in 1955 to £45 million. There was a further increase in this value in 1956, up to approximately £50 million, but as the total value of Hong Kong's exports increased by 26·7 per cent. above the 1955 level, the share of locally manufactured goods declined to about 25 per cent. Textiles became the leading item, occupying approximately 60 per cent. of the total value of locally manufactured goods. Three other important items were footwear, enamel ware, and electric torches. Table 18 (p. 162) shows the relative significance of the various local industries from the export point of view in 1955 and in 1956.[1]

ECONOMIC CONTROLS

In almost all countries, periods of rapid economic development have been associated with rising prices, or at least with inflationary tendencies. In Hong Kong, however, the general level of prices as reflected in the cost-of-living index remained very stable between 1947 and 1950, when a rise occurred due to external reasons, viz. the Korean boom, and thereafter a new stable plateau of prices was reached. As was pointed out earlier,[2] an explanation of this phenomenon can be found in the lack of monetary and credit expansion, the financing of a large part of investment by capital flowing from abroad, unrestricted access to the cheapest foreign sources of supply of producers' and consumers' goods, and the rapidly expanding manufacturing output consisting largely of consumers' goods. A further explanation is to be found in certain price controls which have been at work, especially during the immediate post-war years.[3]

A very important role in the development of Hong Kong's industries has been played by the system of extremely mild trade controls. In order to preserve the Colony's position as a trading centre for South East Asia, the Government has kept trade controls down to a minimum. The war in Korea caused some departure from this policy, as a large number of goods considered to be of strategic importance have been subjected to various forms of control. None the less, the Colony has remained nominally a free port in that there are no general tariff and protective duties. Import and export restrictions for exchange reasons are similar to those in other Commonwealth

---

[1] Hong Kong official statistics do not include all exports of locally manufactured goods, e.g. rattan furniture, sugar, cosmetics, and a number of other items. Thus the value of exports of locally produced goods may be 5–10 per cent. higher than the official figures.

[2] See above, pp. 5–6, 19–20.

[3] Most price controls were introduced by the Military Administration which ruled from 30 August 1945 to May 1946.

territories, and imports from the American/Canadian account area and certain other countries may be financed from the Colony's free market in United States dollars. As a rule, authorization from the exchange control is necessary to pay for all imports from Non-Scheduled Territories.[1] Trade within the Scheduled Territories is normally conducted in sterling or a currency of the Scheduled Territories, and is supervised by the authorized banks, no approval from the exchange control being required. Exchange-control authority is required for remittances unrelated to merchandising, to or from any Scheduled Territory, in a Scheduled Territory currency or in sterling.

All Hong Kong's trade controls are exceedingly simple, especially in comparison with the contemporary restrictionist world. It is here that one of the main keys to the success of Hong Kong's industrial revolution can be found. Almost complete *laissez-faireism* unleashed human potentialities which in other countries have remained paralysed by elaborate control systems. It is particularly in this respect that Benham's opinion applies: 'the remarkable progress achieved . . . merits study by Asian and other countries seeking to develop their manufacturing. The experience of Hong Kong can teach them some valuable lessons, *if they are prepared to learn.*' [2]

The most important measure which helped to keep the cost of living low was the control of rice prices. It was introduced immediately after the end of the war and it lasted for nine years, although towards the end it was practically ineffective. When the control was imposed, rice-rationing tickets were issued. The actual ration varied according to available supplies and fluctuated in 1945–7 from $2\frac{1}{2}$ catties ($3\frac{1}{3}$ lb.) per person per 10 days up to 10 catties ($13\frac{1}{3}$ lb.), the average being about 6 catties (8 lb.).

[1] The Scheduled Territories are the members of the Sterling Area. All other countries are Non-Scheduled Territories and belong either to the American/ Canadian Account Area or to the Transferable Account Area. Imports from countries in the Transferable Account Area are normally financed in transferable sterling or a specified currency. For Indonesia, Cambodia, Laos, Vietnam, China, Taiwan, and Macao finance is usually arranged in Hong Kong dollars. There are no exchange-control formalities for imports from China, Taiwan, and Macao if finance is arranged in Hong Kong dollars. Imports from Thailand are financed in sterling or Hong Kong dollars.

[2] F. C. Benham, 'The Growth of Manufacturing in Hong Kong', *International Affairs*, October 1956, p. 463 (italics are mine).

The Government bought about 60 per cent. of all imported rice and sold it through one wholesaler to retail dealers. Careful watch was kept on the maintenance of stocks so that Hong Kong was never short of rice. However, a large section of the population was excluded from the registration, as the rationing was intended to cover primarily permanent residents of the Colony.

During the immediate post-war period, whenever the rice ration was lowered a supplement of flour was issued. Biscuits and beans were distributed from time to time. Edible oil and peas were issued to the holders of rice cards, butter to those who possessed flour cards (i.e. Europeans), and preserved milk, sugar, and soap to both groups. The system was not confined to foodstuffs. There were occasions when the rice cards were used as a basis for irregular distributions of quilts, blankets, knitting wool, &c. Separate tickets were issued for firewood. In addition, the Government also made efforts to obtain and distribute equitably various raw materials needed by local industries, such as coal, cotton yarn, tin-plate, raw rubber, chemicals, and canvas.

During 1945–7 maximum prices were fixed for a number of commodities, such as flour, peanut oil, salt, sugar, bread, and biscuits. By the end of August 1947 the whole list included about 800 items, but it was mainly restricted to foodstuffs, and such articles as rubber, tobacco, and toilet requisites.[1] Prices of fish and vegetables were never directly controlled, but a marketing system was introduced. Over 95 per cent. of price controls was concerned with imports and, as a rule, prices of locally manufactured goods were not controlled.

The question of completely removing price controls did not arise before September 1947. Soon after this date most of the controls were removed. Rice control was the one which lasted longest; it was finally abandoned in 1954. Before taking this step, however, the Government ensured that the import of rice would be undertaken only by licensed dealers, doing enough business to guarantee the maintenance of ample stocks, i.e. 20 per cent. of annual imports.

In spite of its inevitable defects, rent control, imposed in 1946

---

[1] For full details see D. M. Kenrick, *Price Control and its Practice in Hong Kong* (Hong Kong, Graphic Press, 1954).

and revised in 1949 and again in 1953,[1] partially eased the Colony's housing problem in the immediate post-war years. However, it chiefly benefited the middle classes. The low-paid industrial workers were seldom able to secure rent-controlled accommodation, and in the newly built houses the rent was far above their means. Thus, right from the end of the war, the Colony began to face the very difficult problem of 'squatters', mainly refugees, who used all possible means to secure some kind of shelter, which often hardly deserved this name at all. It is from these miserable squatter huts that a large part of Hong Kong's industrial labour force came forth.

INDUSTRIAL RELATIONS

An almost perfectly elastic labour supply was the main factor explaining the low level of wages, but, in the modern world of trade unionism, it is difficult to understand why there has been such a steady low level of wages in Hong Kong almost throughout the whole post-war decade. In 1955 there were 227 workers' unions, but their economic role was negligible. Personal antagonisms and political considerations divide unions within the same trade. The extent of this division is reflected in the existence of two so-called federations, the Hong Kong Federation of Trade Unions and the Trades Union Council; the former supports the Chinese People's Government in Peking, while the latter favours the Nationalist authorities in Taiwan. There are also some independent unions and a large number of non-unionized workers. As a result, none of the unions is strong enough to affect wage bargaining and conditions of work. The usual method is for the employer to offer a wage and, if the worker finds the terms acceptable, there is an immediate verbal agreement. While there is little unity among workers in the same trade, there is even less among employers, and these agreements can be considered as purely individual. Only in the case of the larger European-managed concerns, such as the public-utility companies and the dockyards, are wages fixed by general agreement, usually with the unions concerned.

There are no official employment exchanges in Hong Kong.

---

[1] *Rent Control in Hong Kong* (Hong Kong, Government Printer, 1953). Abolition or revision of rent control is now under consideration.

F

The traditional method of recruitment is still on the basis of family connexions, personal introductions, and the contractor system. The foreman or chargehand holds himself responsible for the efficiency and good conduct of the men he introduces, who are generally relatives or fellow clansmen. As a result, there have been only very few industrial disputes leading to strikes or lockouts during the whole period of the industrial revolution. On the average, only some 91,000 man-days a year were lost, i.e. about ¼ per cent.

As conditions of work are, on the whole, safe and healthy, there have been very few industrial accidents and injuries. The accident rate averaged about 5·6 per thousand workers in 1950–5, and the incidence of fatalities was only 0·187 p.a. per thousand workers during the same period. In December 1953 the Workmen's Compensation Ordinance was introduced. In the medical and health fields much is being done by the Government and by charitable and philanthropic bodies. The Government operates 2 general hospitals, 2 maternity hospitals, a social-hygiene hospital, and a mental hospital. Charitable and religious organizations are responsible for some 8 hospitals and a TB sanatorium. Clinics are established in all the larger factories, and some of them employ a full-time doctor as well. Several trade unions, and many voluntary welfare bodies, operate their own clinics. All this, however, is very little in comparison with needs, so that medical facilities in the Colony are far from adequate. Fortunately, no industrial diseases exist in Hong Kong. The normal diet of the working-class Chinese is well balanced and, since the traditional methods of cooking preserve the full nutritional value of food, deficiency diseases are also rare. There is a widespread habit of eating at restaurants, tea-shops, canteens, or street stalls, where for 50 cents a substantial meal is obtainable. In smaller concerns it is customary for the employer to provide meals free on the premises and to eat together with his family and employees.

This habit of eating away from home has not only reduced the cost of food, but has also relieved many women of household duties and enabled them to take up industrial employment. As much as 37 per cent. of the industrial labour force consists of women, and in some branches they are almost exclusively employed. They are paid about 30 per cent. less than men, and most of them are on daily or piece rates. This has contributed to the success of many light industries. Fairly large numbers of women are also employed as earth carriers in construction work.

The employment of women between 8 p.m. and 7 a.m., and of children under the age of 14 years, in any industrial undertaking is prohibited by law; but youngsters just over 14 work in a large variety of industries. In 1955, 1,445 young persons between the ages of 14 and 18 years were registered by the Labour Department; of this number 1,003 were girls.

Apprenticeship is common in Chinese-run establishments, but it is loosely organized, with little or no technical instruction and no rationalized system of training, so that the apprentice is expected to pick up his skill by watching and imitating. But a number of large industrial establishments have well developed apprenticeship systems, those of the Taikoo Dockyard & Engineering Co. and the Hongkong & Whampoa Dock Co. being of particular note. In 1954 a training programme for technical personnel in the textile trade was initiated by the South Sea Textile Manufacturing Co.; this example has been followed by some other large enterprises.

Two large private institutions under the management of Salesian Fathers provide technical training for boys. The Aberdeen Trade School offers instruction in shoemaking, tailoring, printing, and book-binding, and the Tang King Po School holds courses for mechanics, electricians, and carpenters. Classes in engineering and radio communication are run by a number of small private schools, while the Far Eastern Flying Training School prepares students for examination in these subjects as well as in flying. Many voluntary welfare societies run classes in various handicrafts, embroidery, and dressmaking.

The Hong Kong Technical College is the principal government institution for training in mechanical engineering, building, telecommunications, navigation, and commerce. Technical training for girls is provided by the government-owned Ho Tung Technical School for Girls, where courses are offered in art, handicraft, cookery, dressmaking, and embroidery. The Evening Institute of the Education Department holds classes in English, handiwork, carpentry, knitting, sewing, &c. Commercial subjects are taught in a number of private evening schools and in the Evening School of the Hong Kong General Chamber of Commerce. So far, no commercial courses have been given in the University of Hong Kong except an experimental extramural course instituted in 1956, but there are Civil Engineering and Architecture Departments, besides a number of Arts and Science Departments and a well established Faculty of Medicine.

Again, all these facilities are quite inadequate when compared with needs. Much therefore remains to be done in the field of technical education, on which the future of Hong Kong industries chiefly depends.

THE HUMAN ELEMENT

So far, almost all the Colony's expanding industries have been labour-intensive and the cost of labour has been low. Official statistics reveal that the daily wages during 1953–5 were HK\$6·00–8·50 (7s. 6d.–10s. 7½d.) for skilled workers, HK\$5·00–6·50 (6s. 3d.–8s. 1½d.) for semi-skilled, and HK\$3·00—5·00 (3s. 9d.–6s. 3d.) for unskilled workers.[1] In many industries, particularly in building and construction, wages were, in fact, much below this level. However, consideration should be given to the custom of paying the Chinese New Year bonus (normally amounting to one month's earnings), overtime payments, food and accommodation supplements, and the fact that some labourers work for more than one factory, particularly in the garment industry, by sometimes taking another shift in a different establishment.

More illuminating, therefore, would be an estimate of average monthly earnings. According to a sample survey of industrial workers' earnings and expenditure carried out by the present writer in December 1955,[2] an average industrial family was earning HK\$264 a month. Of this sum 80·7 per cent., i.e. HK\$213, was contributed by the head of the household, and the rest was earned by the remaining members of the family. This would give about HK\$66 (or approximately £4) per head per month, and about £3 a week earned by the chief supporter of the family. Thus in comparison with Britain, where in December 1955 the average weekly earnings of industrial

---

[1] Commissioner of Labour, *Annual Departmental Report, 1954–5*, p. 28.
[2] Szczepanik, *Cost of Living*, p. 5.

workers amounted to about £9 a week,[1] the Hong Kong worker
was earning only one-third as much as his British counterpart.
Allowance should be made, however, for the difference in the
cost of living and expenditure pattern in the two countries.
Table 19 (p. 163) serves this purpose.

The effect of a lower level of wages in Hong Kong was
mainly reflected in a higher percentage of expenditure on food
and beverages. Hong Kong workers, therefore, have not been
starving. On the contrary, if it is considered that the cost of
simple food in Hong Kong is much cheaper, and that the warm
climate does not require such a large calorie intake as in
Britain, it could be concluded that the industrial revolution in
Hong Kong was not taking place at the expense of the standards
of nutrition. The Hong Kong worker, moreover, was spending
much less on smoking than the British worker, and the geographical limitation of the Colony's area did not require so
much to be spent on transport as in Britain. The main hard-
ships of Hong Kong workers are to be found in the very low
housing standards. Expenditure on rent in the Colony was
relatively higher than in Britain, and the standard of accommodation obtainable was much lower; especially if it is considered
that only about 1 per cent. of the worker's budget was spent on
household equipment, whereas in the United Kingdom the
corresponding percentage was 6·6.

However, a comparison between present conditions in Hong
Kong and the United Kingdom may not be quite appropriate.
If means were available, it would be more proper to compare
workers' standards of living in Hong Kong in the early 1950s
and in the United Kingdom in the middle of the nineteenth
century when the British industrial take-off occurred. It would
be most instructive also to compare Hong Kong with Communist China, where planned industrialization was commenced almost simultaneously. Unfortunately, scarcity of
statistical data only permits comparison of some basic items.
According to available information, the average monthly earnings of an industrial worker, e.g. in a state cotton mill, in China
amount to 52 *yüan*. Assuming that he spends, as in Hong Kong,
53·8 per cent. of his wage on food, his total food expenditure
would be 28 *yüan* per month. Table 20 (p. 163) shows the

[1] *The Economist*, 29 December 1956.

quantities of the basic foodstuffs which he would be able to buy each month, if he tried to distribute this sum in the same way as a Hong Kong worker. This comparison shows that the standard of living of industrial workers in Hong Kong, low as it is, is much higher than in China. This explains why the Colony has been constantly receiving, apart from political refugees, an inflow of economic immigrants from the mainland. Compared with Communist China, the industrial revolution in the capitalistic Colony of Hong Kong has been taking place in much more humanitarian conditions. Our analysis also shows that it would be highly unfair to accuse Hong Kong's industrialization of causing misery among the workers. The economic system of Hong Kong, with its powerful mechanism of competition which keeps all prices low, not only enables the workers to maintain a fairly decent standard of living, but also permits an average family to save some 2·35 per cent. of its monthly earnings,[1] and to send another part of these earnings to relatives in China.

When considering the level of wages in Hong Kong, the length of the working day must be taken into account. Broadly speaking, an 8-hour day is worked by government, by European, and by some Chinese concerns. But the majority of Chinese concerns work longer hours, particularly when orders are plentiful, and a 10-hour day is almost the rule, 12 hours not being uncommon. Alternatively, spinning mills, three of which also operate weaving sheds, work on an 8-hour shift system, with women on the day shifts and men on both day and night shifts. According to a recent survey compiled by the International Federation of Cotton and Allied Textile Industries, in 1955–6 Hong Kong spindles operated for 8,522 hours out of a year's total of 8,784 hours. Contrasted with this top position of Hong Kong, Indian spindles worked 5,602 hours, Dutch 4,308 hours, German 3,729 hours, French 3,325 hours, whereas the Lancashire mills were at the bottom of the list with only 1,526 hours.[2]

This system, which is also employed in some other industries, results in a high degree of capital-utilization. It is here that another aspect of the secret of successful industrialization can be found. Hong Kong manufacturers boast that they are

[1] Szczepanik, *Cost of Living*, p. 5.
[2] *Reuters*, 22 February 1957.

obtaining from abroad the most modern machinery in the cheapest market, and operating it three times as intensively as in most Western countries. As a result, neither capital nor labour is allowed to be left idle.

Officially, there are sixteen general holidays during the year in Hong Kong, in addition to Sundays. But these holidays are granted with pay only by the Government, the banks, and most European-managed companies and business houses. Only a few large Chinese-managed concerns grant a weekly or regular periodic holiday to all their workers. The majority of smaller Chinese shops, factories, and workshops only grant holidays at the Chinese New Year, at *Ching Ming*, and at a few other festivals, especially those connected with the trade or industry itself. Thus Sundays are very seldom observed, and as a result work in the Colony goes on almost without interruption *the whole year round*, often without machines stopping even at night. All this produces a picture of intense vitality which impresses any visitor to the Colony.

THE MECHANISM OF INDUSTRIAL GROWTH

The preceding part of this study examined the motivating forces, the institutional structure, and the historical reasons for Hong Kong's post-war economic growth. The next task is to ascertain the causal mechanism of this development. It appears that it was essentially of double character.

On the one hand, there emerged a heavy pressure of *internal demand* resulting from the primary wants of shelter, clothing, and food, as well as from wants of a higher order, such as education, entertainment, or adornment. Apart from the rapidly growing number of the Colony's civilian residents, additional demand was due to the increased British garrison, and to the continuous stream of numerous United States naval and military personnel for whom Hong Kong was selected as a Far Eastern leave centre. Finally, further stimulus was given by the growing number of tourists. The economy, once stimulated by a series of manifold intensive shocks, began to respond cumulatively to various complementary and derived demands so that its entire infrastructure was affected and a fairly well-balanced over-all development followed.

On the other hand, a new *external demand* had arisen for a

number of similar goods, particularly in the neighbouring countries of South East Asia. The commercial connexions of the Colony's entrepôt network have carried overseas a large part of its manufactured output, in some cases as much as 90 per cent., and on the average at least 40 per cent. In connexion with this, a favourable influence was exerted by the system of imperial preference and by the temporary absence of Japanese competition. Of great importance also was the politico-historical factor which has singled out Hong Kong as an almost exclusive supplier of 'things Chinese', not only in the material sense, such as carved furniture, silk brocades, or preserved ginger, but also in the cultural sense, in the form of books, periodicals, journals, and Chinese films.

The United Kingdom has always been Hong Kong's best customer, with orders in 1956 amounting to 21 per cent. of the total value of locally produced goods sold abroad. But next in importance were various African countries (18 per cent. of the total in 1956), then Indonesia (16 per cent.), and Malaya (11 per cent.). These four major importers took up about 66 per cent. of the total value of Hong Kong exports of locally manufactured goods in 1956. Other Far Eastern countries (Thailand, Indochina, the Philippines) followed these four. Table 21 (p. 164), illustrates the detailed position in this respect in 1955 and 1956.

Arising from these two sources of demand, local and foreign, it became possible to undertake production for a fairly large market. This facilitated various economies of scale, both internal and external, and helped to keep down commodity prices already cheap on account of the low labour cost. As a result, the economy became remarkably competitive.

When considering the mechanism of Hong Kong's industrial revolution, a distinction should be made between the following four broad industrial groups:

1. The first comprises all the industries forming the infrastructure of the economy: shipbuilding and ship repairing; aircraft maintenance and repair; railway workshops; maintenance and repairs for internal marine and land transport; and public utilities, especially electricity and gas. The growth of this group of industries gave rise to the construction of diesel engines, and the manufacture of rope and nets, nails, screws, hinges,

wire, &c. Although all these industries developed around the port and entrepôt activities of the Colony, they proved sufficiently responsive to the demands of the growing population and of manufacturing industry. In 1955 they accounted for about 15 per cent. of employment in the registered factories and workshops. This first group of industries will be discussed in Chapter 7.

2. The housing and construction boom gave rise to the expansion of the cement and allied industries; the rolling of steel bars; the production of drilling machines and water pumps, plumbing, fittings, and tubes; as well as the manufacture of glass, chemicals (especially paints), furniture, metal products, and electrical apparatus and appliances. Indirectly, this development stimulated the growth of the Colony's machine industry. This whole group of industries absorbed about 27 per cent. of Hong Kong's labour force employed in the registered establishments, not counting the building and construction industry itself. The analysis of this second group of industries will be carried out in Chapter 8.

3. Just as the primary need for shelter stimulated the growth of a number of industries, the demand for clothing and food gave impetus to the development of the manufacture of textiles, rubber and leather footwear, and food and beverages. In subtropical climatic conditions, food and beverage consumption led to the growth of the ice and cold-storage industry. All these industries, which will be examined in Chapter 9, absorbed about 48 per cent. of the Colony's labour force employed in the registered factories and workshops.

4. Finally, there has been a marked increase in the demand resulting from various secondary and tertiary wants, such as education, entertainment, and adornment. It is here that the cultural impact of the free mixing of western and eastern civilizations became very pronounced. One of the most interesting developments in this field was the growth of the plastics industry transplanted from the West, and the manufacture of such goods as plastic tooth-brushes, fountain pens, and even cameras. The expansion of the printing, publishing, and film industries was the effect of the direct response of the economy to the increasing demand for cultural services and goods. Last but not least, this group includes the industries which developed

in connexion with tourism, facilitated by the ease of modern travel and communication. This fourth group of industries, which will be examined in Chapter 10, absorbed about 10 per cent. of the Colony's labour employed in the registered factories and workshops, not counting the tailoring, hotel, and catering industries.

7

The Adaptation of the Infrastructure

THE study of the development of the Colony's infrastructure—the port, transport, communications, and public utilities—shows its remarkable adaptation to the rate of economic growth after the war. Graphs III and IV indicate that the expansion of the infrastructure was very rapid between 1948 and 1951. The rate of growth between 1951 and 1953 was, on the whole, smaller, and in some cases there was even a decline in the volume of services provided. From 1953 onwards a new expansionary phase followed, but in some fields there were signs of a need for more radical changes in the nature and scope of the public-utility services.[1] Some of these changes are already taking place.

THE PORT OF HONG KONG

Thanks to advantages of location, Hong Kong soon became one of the main ports of South China and later of the Far East. The port is the focal point of the bulk of economic activities, and the transport network radiating from it has contributed greatly to the expansion of exports of Hong Kong's own industrial products.

The long water-fronts on each side of the natural harbour have provided ample accommodation for docks, wharves, and warehouses. The depth of the water is sufficient for all types of ship, while the surrounding hills keep it well sheltered. The small tidal range allows ships to come and go at any time, and the ease of entry makes piloting almost unnecessary. These natural advantages, together with a cheap-labour supply, have contributed largely to keeping harbourage dues low. Faithful to its traditionally liberal economic policy, the Government has not tried to use the harbour as a significant source of revenue and has not interfered with its natural economic development,

[1] For a fuller discussion of this matter see my article on the 'Economics of Public Utilities in Hong Kong', *Far East. Econ. R.*, 29 December 1955.

GRAPH III

Post-war Development of Shipping and Air Transport

(*1947–8 = 100*)

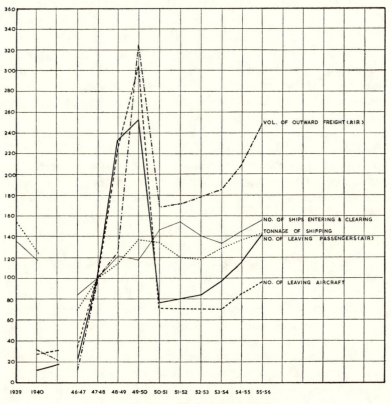

Source: Tables 22 and 23, Statistical Appendix.

leaving it mainly to private enterprise, under the general control of the Marine Department. Even pilotage is not compulsory.

The existing commercial piers, wharves, and godowns are
operated by four private enterprises. The oldest and largest
of these, the Hongkong & Kowloon Wharf & Godown Co.,
provides 6 berths for 10 ocean-going vessels and 1 coastal vessel,
and operates over 100 godowns with a total storage space of

GRAPH IV

The Growth of Internal Transport and Public Utility Services

$(1948 = 100)$

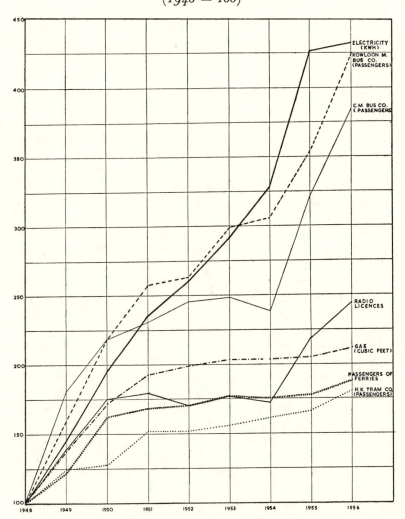

Source: Tables 24, 26, 28, 30 and 32, Statistical Appendix.

500,000 measurement tons. A railway siding connects the Company's main premises with the Kowloon–Canton Railway. Holt's Wharf, situated near the terminal of the Kowloon–Canton Railway, is operated mainly for ships of the Blue Funnel Line and Glen Line. It has two deep-water berths and storage space for about 46,000 tons. China Provident Loan & Mortgage Co. provides storage space for about 175,000 tons but does not operate any moorings or piers. In connexion with post-war economic development, North Point Wharfs Co. was incorporated in 1948. It has 1,220 feet of quayage in the industrial district of North Point on the Island, and its present storage and transit capacity is 60,000 tons. In addition, there are about 100 Chinese-owned small godowns with a total storage capacity of 350,000 tons. Thus the aggregate storage capacity of Hong Kong godowns is estimated at 1 million tons.

Ships arriving in the harbour either proceed to piers and wharves, or anchor in midstream to load or unload. Suggestions were made that if the Government provided more piers and wharves having direct access to warehouses, greater efficiency would result. So far, these suggestions have not been adopted. One beneficial aspect of this policy is the maintenance of a source of income for a large number of crews serving about 20,000 miscellaneous small junks and harbour boats available for handling cargo and for transport between ships at buoys and the shore. In addition, one large and two smaller companies provide water for the ships.

There are twenty shipbuilding and ship repairing establishments in the Colony, employing between them about 7,000 workers. The two main dockyards are the Hongkong & Whampoa Dock Co., and the Taikoo Dockyard & Engineering Co., which together are capable of producing 80,000 tons of new vessels (up to 10,000 tons capacity) a year. Vessels up to 500 feet in length can be accommodated in their building berths. Shipbuilding and ship repairing constitute the most important part of the Colony's heavy industry and a significant line of exports which, in the post-war period, included deliveries to Korea and several other neighbouring countries, particularly Thailand, North Borneo, and the Philippines.

The Japanese occupation caused great damage to port facilities. Moreover, shipping was depleted and in poor condition. In spite of this, by the end of 1946 ships were already entering and leaving Hong Kong freely, and shipping repairs and even shipbuilding had begun. Table 22 (p. 165) and Graph III illustrate the post-war recovery of the port. From 1946 to 1950 the number of vessels entering the port and the tonnage were steadily increasing, but between 1950 and 1953, owing to the embargo, there was a decline in the tonnage of ships handled. From 1953 onwards, however, a definite improvement began. In 1954–5 the tonnage reached the 1949–50 post-war peak, although not the 1939 level. By the summer of 1956 almost all godowns were full and even some shortage of labour in the harbour was experienced. This was due to new directions in entrepôt trade, the growth of local manufacturing industry, and the relaxation of political tension. Quick response to the pressure of these factors is a proof of the great vitality and flexibility of Hong Kong's harbour and all the industries connected with it.

Although Hong Kong's economic development has depended primarily on its marine port, in recent years its airport has assumed an ever-growing importance. A small military airfield was opened in 1924, but its use for civil aviation began in 1930 when the first flights were made to Canton. In 1936 the Government constructed an airport at Kai Tak, situated on the mainland about 4 miles from the centre of Kowloon, which in a very short time became the terminal point for a number of airlines. At the end of the war the airport was devastated, but it was soon rehabilitated to receive aircraft of all the major airlines of the world. In 1950 the main paved runway was extended by a further 200 yards, which proved to be the limit of expansion. In 1955 work began on the new airport. The plans provide for constructing a promontory 800 feet wide and 8,300 feet in length, containing a 7,200-foot paved runway. The whole, consisting of about 160 acres, will be a consolidated reclamation from the sea. The hills in the approach to the runway are being demolished to provide a larger clearance angle, and the material is being used as part of the filling material for the reclamation. The new runway will be brought into use towards the end of 1958, and the new terminal area should be ready by late 1959. The whole cost will amount to £6 million. In the design of the scheme, consideration was given to the possible recoupment of about half of the capital expenditure by the disposal of some 160 acres of the existing airport.[1]

Graph III and Table 23 (p. 165) illustrate the development of aviation in Hong Kong from 1946 to 1956. The cessation of services to the mainland of China in 1950 resulted in a considerable decrease in traffic. Nevertheless, after a heavy decline in 1950–1, the volume of traffic has been steadily increasing and the growth of outward freight and mail has been very conspicuous.

By 1956 the number of companies operating regular air transport via Hong Kong increased to fifteen. The largest number of passengers is carried by Pan American World Airways. BOAC occupies the third place, the second being taken by the local company Cathay Pacific Airways, which was formed soon after the end of the war and has developed from small beginnings into an important regional airline of high reputation. It operates services to Manila, Singapore, Bangkok, Rangoon, Calcutta, Saigon, and North Borneo. Cathay Pacific Airways was established by an American–Australian partnership and bought in 1949 by Butterfield & Swire. Hong Kong Airways, founded in 1948 for local services to China, suspended operations in 1949, but was reopened in 1957 by Jardine, Matheson, the second leading commercial house of the colony, with services to Manila and Seoul, BOAC providing half the capital.

Just as the seaport gave rise to the development of shipbuilding and repairing, the growth of air transport stimulated the formation in Hong Kong of an important centre for the maintenance, repair, and overhaul of aircraft operating in the Far East. Two firms were set up for this purpose after the war. One, Jardine Aircraft Maintenance Co., was started by Jardine, Matheson with initial technical assistance from BOAC. The second, Pacific Air Maintenance & Supply Co., was launched by Butterfield & Swire, with Australian National Airways holding an interest. In 1950 an agreement was reached to merge both these into the Hong Kong Aircraft Engineering Co. It provides full servicing facilities for all commercial aircraft passing through Hong Kong. In addition, aircraft, engines, propellers,

[1] The Inter-departmental Committee on the New Airport did not accept this consideration, as it was based on offsetting the value of land released against the cost of reclamation, no value being placed on the sea-bed.

accessories, and instruments are sent for overhaul from countries as far afield as New Guinea, India, and Korea. The Far East Flying Training School maintains facilities for the repair of small aircraft, in addition to the training of engineers and flying crews. All these services challenge comparison with any in the world, and are unrivalled on the western side of the Pacific.

INTERNAL TRANSPORT

Hong Kong is a mountainous area with sheer cliffs and jutting spurs. These conditions are not conducive to road building, and a large amount of blasting and cutting has been necessary in order to lay road foundations. Climatic conditions make maintenance difficult, as the torrential summer rains often cause serious damage to road surfaces. In spite of this, there is a good road system, which in 1956 consisted of 450 miles: 185 miles on the Island, 122 in Kowloon, and 143 in the New Territories. These figures clearly indicate the relative scarcity of roads in the New Territories, which occupy about 90 per cent. of the total area of the Colony but contain only 30 per cent. of the road length. Further economic growth of Hong Kong would need to include an extensive programme of road building in the New Territories to open them up for housing, agriculture, industry, &c. To make the road density in the New Territories equal to that on the Island, something like 1,900 miles of new roads would have to be built. At present, only 6 or 7 miles of new public roads are added each year.

Even on the Island of Hong Kong, road building has been very slow. Until motor roads were opened in 1924, the Peak Tramway, founded in 1888 and first known as the Hong Kong High Level Tramway, was almost the only means of access to the Peak area, and contributed much to its development. At present, as Peak residents usually own private cars, it mainly serves workers, servants, school children, and week-enders. As the route goes up to a point on Victoria Peak 1,300 feet above sea-level, it is an important attraction to tourists.

A much more important tram service is provided by the Hongkong Tramway Co., which in 1956 was running 138 cars on a track of about 19½ miles in the urban district of Victoria. It operates under a concession (incorporated in the 1902 Ordinance) calling for a royalty payment at the rate of 25 per

G

cent. of annual net profits. This royalty amounts to about HK$1¾ million a year.

The bus services are provided by the Kowloon Motor Bus Co. on the Mainland and the China Motor Bus Co. on the Island. Both are private companies operating under special franchises. The royalty paid by the Kowloon Motor Bus Co. is about HK$6 million and the royalty paid by the China Motor Bus Co. amounts to HK$2 million a year.

Graph IV and Table 24 (p. 166) illustrate the services rendered by bus and tramway companies during 1948–56, and indicate a particularly rapid growth of the services provided by the bus companies which proved to be very responsive to the increase in demand.

Since the end of the war there has been a large increase in the number of motor vehicles in Hong Kong. In 1956 about 29,000 vehicles of all kinds were registered. This results in a density of sixty-three vehicles per mile of roadway, causing congestion and bottlenecks, especially in the rush hours. With the increase in motor traffic, the repair of motor vehicles and cycles became a rapidly developing industry. There are now six well equipped modern garages operated by the motor-vehicle agencies and a number of smaller ones engaged in engine maintenance and repairs. The two bus companies and the tramway company have large workshops, but these are solely engaged in the overhauling and body-building of their own vehicles. Several thousand people find employment as car cleaners and car-park watchmen.

The Kowloon–Canton Railway, the only railway in the Colony, is government-owned. The British section of this railway, from Kowloon to the border town of Lowu, is only 22 miles long. The Kowloon station is the southern terminus of a railway system, inaugurated in 1910, running between Kowloon, Canton, Hankow, and Shanghai, with connexions from these cities to north China and Europe. Since the Communist Government took over the administration of Canton late in 1949, passengers travelling to and from the interior have had to change trains at the border. Goods traffic in wagon loads, however, operates without off-loading; only small consignments in incomplete wagon loads have had to be unloaded and carried over the frontier.

Shortening the route of the railway and the increase in its use for internal transport necessitated a gradual change to diesel traction; and over HK$10 million has been spent on this in the three years 1954–6. Even with its present limitations, the railway brought some HK$3·8 million of operating profit to the Government in 1956. The railway workshops form an important part of the Colony's heavy industry. They suffered greatly by looting and damage during the war, but rehabilitation was rapid and is now complete. They are well equipped and capable of carrying out all railway repairs; and they do much work for other government departments.

Table 25 (p. 166) illustrates the volume of services rendered by the railway in the post-war period. Since 1950 both passenger and goods transport have declined heavily. The present volume of traffic is maintained near the 1947–8 level, thanks mainly to the increase in internal traffic; in 1955 passengers carried within the territory of the Colony formed about 93 per cent. of the total. Although in 1956 the number of passengers crossing the border increased to 24 per cent. of the total, the railway will not regain its former prosperity until there is a relaxation of the trade and travel restrictions now in force between Hong Kong and China.

Transport services between Hong Kong, Kowloon, and the various islands in the New Territories are provided by ferries operated by two independent companies: the Star Ferry Co. and the Hongkong and Yaumati Ferry Co. The Star Ferry Co., established in the 1890s, now operates under an Ordinance, revised in 1951, which gives the Company the sole right to maintain the ferry service for fifteen years, from 1950 onwards, with the possibility of further renewal of the concession. The Company operates only one route between the southern end of the Kowloon peninsula and the water-front of Victoria City, a distance of approximately 1 mile. The Company pays pier rent at the rate of HK$15,000 per month, and a royalty at a progressive rate varying from 5 per cent., if the monthly receipts amount to HK$200,000, up to 15 per cent. if they reach HK$500,000. This royalty brings in about HK$500,000 each year, and its effective incidence amounts to 25 per cent. of the Company's net profit.

The Hongkong & Yaumati Ferry Co. was founded in 1924

with only eleven small wooden boats to run three cross-harbour routes. The routes to other parts of the mainland and the neighbouring islands were added later, and in 1932 the vehicular ferry was introduced. These vehicular and outlying-districts services contributed a great deal to the development of the New Territories, particularly the islands of Cheung Chau and Lantao. By 1956 the Company had forty-six vessels in operation and maintained six cross-harbour services as well as ferry services to the outlying districts in the New Territories. The Ferry operates under the 1953 Ordinance, which gives the Company the exclusive right to maintain services for fifteen years from 1950 onwards, and thereafter renewable. The Company pays pier rent at HK$45,000 per month and a royalty equal to 25 per cent. of net annual profits, which brings in about HK$2 million to the Government.

Graph IV and Table 26 (p. 167) illustrate the volume of services rendered by the two ferry companies in the post-war period. It appears that since 1950 there has been only a comparatively small increase in the number of passengers carried. A greater separation of Kowloon as an economic and social entity may be one of the reasons for this. It is likely, however, that the number of ferry passengers could be made greater through a bold investment programme aiming at a substantial increase in the number of ferries, piers, traffic-dispersal platforms, &c., as well as in the number of passenger and goods routes. It seems that even with the existing pattern of geographical distribution of the Colony's population, the present system of internal marine transport calls for revision. Assuming the inevitability of expansion of the population to numerous islands which at present are almost deserted, imaginative planning of the future transport network becomes a necessity. If the ferry companies fail to fulfil this role it is possible that alternative means of internal transport—tunnels, bridges, causeways, or helicopters—will have to be introduced.

BROADCASTING, POST OFFICE, AND TELECOMMUNICATIONS

Tables 27 and 28 (pp. 167, 168), illustrate the rapid growth of services rendered by the government-owned Post Office and Radio Hong Kong. Rediffusion (Hong Kong), is a private enterprise operating a wired-broadcasting system under a franchise granted in 1948, and providing programmes in English and in Chinese. The programmes include relays from Radio Hong Kong, the BBC, and other stations, but most of them originate in the Company's own studios. The distribution network, which at the beginning of 1954 covered the whole of the urban areas of Victoria and Kowloon and most of the Peak, has recently been extended to the New Territories. Altogether some 53,000 loudspeakers had been installed by the end of 1954. Each subscriber pays a service rental charge of HK$10.00 per month and an additional HK$5.00 a month for an extra point. The Company pays the Government a radio licence fee of HK$20 a year in respect of each subscriber.

Under an Ordinance revised in 1955, the Hong Kong Telephone Co., a private enterprise, has the sole right of supplying telephone services in the Colony for fifty years from 1925. It pays a royalty equal to 25 per cent. of net annual profits, which amounts to about HK$750,000, and a majority of its directors must be British subjects. Subscriptions, which are charged on a flat scale, are HK$225 a year for residential, and HK$300 for business, subscribers. In 1941 the Company had 19,100 lines. By 1956 the number of direct telephone lines had increased to 45,000 and, with 18,500 extensions, the total number of subscribers amounted to 63,500. In spite of this increase, the Company cannot yet meet all the public demand for its services.

Cable and Wireless, a branch of the nationalized British company operating under a special franchise, was in 1956 maintaining telecommunications and radio-telephone services to sixty-one countries. The Company provides a service for internal telegrams throughout the Colony, and is responsible for the technical maintenance and development of Hong Kong's broadcasting and Aeradio services, meteorological radio services, and the VHF communications of various government departments.

PUBLIC UTILITIES

The Colony's water supply is under the control of the Public Works Department. There are no large rivers or underground sources of water, and Hong Kong has to depend on the collection of rain-water in reservoirs between May and September.

There is little rain during the remainder of the year. In 1956 the total capacity of the existing thirteen storage reservoirs was 5,970 million gallons, of which 2,362 million were on the Island. Of the remaining 3,608 million gallons on the mainland, 2,921 were contained in the Jubilee Reservoirs at Shing Mun near Tsun Wan. The water from reservoirs situated in the New Territories is conveyed across the harbour in two submarine pipes. A large proportion of the water has to be pumped. All water is filtered and chlorinated and the supplies metered. The present price is 80 cents per 1,000 gallons for domestic use or industry, and HK$2 per 1,000 gallons for shipping or constructional purposes.

Table 29 (p. 168) illustrates the volume of water consumption in the Colony in the post-war period. The large post-war increase in the population has resulted in a demand which is well in excess of the available resources, and has necessitated restrictions in the hours of supply, sometimes to two hours a day. In 1957 basic work was completed on a new system of reservoirs in Tai Lam Chung Valley. These reservoirs will impound 4,500 million gallons. It is estimated, however, that even the addition of the Tai Lam Chung reservoirs will not solve the problem. Tests are therefore being made to construct a new reservoir in the Shek Pik Valley on Lantao Island.

In 1861 the Hong Kong & China Gas Co. was established to supply gas on Hong Kong Island. This service was extended to the mainland in 1892. Until recently, this Company was a subsidiary of the London Gas Board, and the shares were all handled in London. In 1954 a majority of the shares was acquired by a large holding company in Hong Kong, which involved a change in the management and the transfer of the head office to Hong Kong. The Company has no special licence and is subject to ordinary business-profits taxes.

Graph IV and Table 30 (p. 169) illustrate the post-war growth of gas output. The gas manufactured and distributed among about 9,320 consumers in 1956 was approximately 600 million cubic feet. Of this only about 10 per cent. was for industrial purposes and for public lighting, and the rest was for domestic use. But, owing to its high cost as compared with other fuels, only a small number of homes, mainly European, are equipped with it. The scale of charges varies from HK$13·00 per 1,000 cubic feet on the first 10,000 cubic feet to HK$11·50 per 1,000 cubic feet for consumption exceeding 50,000 cubic feet. For industrial purposes gas can hardly compete with electricity, which is also gradually taking its place in public lighting.

Electricity in Hong Kong was first supplied in 1889, when the Hong Kong Electric Co. was incorporated. In 1941 its generating capacity was 54,000 kw.; by the end of 1955 this had increased to 92,500 kw., and in 1956 the annual output amounted to 272 million kwh. This Company supplies electricity only on the Island, whereas on the mainland it is supplied by the China Light & Power Co. There is also a small enterprise, Cheung Chau Electric Co., which supplies electricity in Cheung Chau. The China Light & Power Co., registered in 1901 to supply Canton, opened a station at Kowloon in 1903. After the sale of its plant and equipment in Canton in 1909, its business was confined to the Kowloon peninsula. It paid no regular dividend till 1930, by which time its capital had gradually been raised from HK$300,000 to HK$10 million. At present its authorized capital stands at HK$100 million, HK$42 million of which has been issued. Between 1913 and 1956 the area served has increased from 2 square miles with 670 customers to over 200 square miles with about 80,000, and its annual output from 500,000 to about 380 million kwh.

The two electricity companies have no monopoly rights, and thus pay only ordinary business-profits taxes. Electricity supply is regulated by the Ordinance of 1911, which deals essentially with safety measures. Table 31 (p. 169) shows the charges of the two companies in 1941, 1946, and 1955. A phenomenon deserving special attention is a considerable fall in charges between 1946 and 1955. This was due to a very large increase in output, which is shown in Graph IV and Table 32 (p. 170). Within less than seventy years, the two companies have developed to such an extent that their output *per capita* is only below that of Japan among all the East Asian countries. In 1956 the total production of electricity in Hong Kong was about 650 million kwh., i.e. *per capita* consumption amounted to approximately 270 kwh. p.a. With new and improved equipment and thermo-generating plants the two companies meet the present demand adequately. Hong Kong is probably the only place in the Far East to have had no post-war power shortage, in spite of the increase in consumption. The expansion of electricity production may be regarded as the best example of the adaptability of Hong Kong's infrastructure to the demands of industrialization.

8

The Impact of the Housing Boom

CONSTRUCTION AND BUILDING INDUSTRY

ONE of the most conspicuous developmental factors in Hong Kong was the growth of the construction and building industry which absorbed a large part of the capital flowing from abroad and formed internally in the Colony. Table 33 (p. 170) illustrates the magnitude of this investment between 1948 and 1956. On the average, it amounted to about HK$140 million per annum, i.e. approximately 5 per cent. of the national income. The significance of this investment can be better appreciated if it is contrasted with the value of all pre-war buildings in March 1948, which was estimated at HK$200 million.[1] Thus, with allowance for depreciation, approximately one-half of the existing capital value of buildings was added and some 900–1,000 new buildings were constructed every year, 50–60 per cent. for domestic purposes. In view of the scarcity of building sites and the constant rise in the price of land,[2] the policy has been to pull down old buildings, and extend upwards by adding to the number of stories, instead of extending sideways. Even for resettlement purposes, the Government has abandoned the erection of cottages and has taken to building multi-story blocks.

The growth of the building and construction industry was greatly favoured by the abundance and cheapness of labour. Basic wages are extremely low, as is indicated in Table 35 (p. 171). According to official estimates, about 250,000 persons were employed in this industry in 1954–5.[3] This figure seems to be highly exaggerated, but without special investigation it is impossible to define the degree of error. Unionized labour amounted to only 10,000.

The cheapness of labour also explains the comparatively low

[1] Ma and Szczepanik, *National Income*, p. 53.
[2] See Table 34, p. 171.
[3] Commissioner of Labour, *Annual Departmental Report, 1954–5*, p. 12. My guess is that this industry gave employment to about 100,000 persons.

degree of mechanization. The machines most commonly employed are pile-driving machines, concrete mixers, and vibrators. Whenever manual labour is possible, it is used. Only some of the raw materials are supplied locally, i.e. sand, granite, and bricks. Cement manufactured locally is also available, but supply has never been able to meet demand.[1] Immediately after the war, cement was imported from Australia, later from Japan, and more recently from China. Tiles, steel bars, water pipes, and ironmongery are mainly imported from the United Kingdom, and partly from other European countries and the United States; timber is brought from Malaya, North Borneo, Burma, and Thailand.

Immediately after the war there were many small speculative construction companies which depended upon the quick sale of buildings to finance their projects. In addition to high rents, there was a widespread custom of demanding considerable key money, so that loans for speculative dealings in houses could be repaid within $3\frac{1}{2}$–4 years. Money-lenders and even some banks were usually ready to grant loans with land as security at a rate of interest fluctuating from 5–6 per cent. for the banks to 12–18 per cent. p.a. for money-lenders. Raw materials were obtainable on credit. This type of speculation has recently considerably diminished, and many smaller construction firms have disappeared or been amalgamated.

In 1955 the rate of profit in the industry varied between 5 and 15 per cent. of the total cost of construction. This was regarded as an indication that the demand for high-rent housing had reached a point of saturation, and the number of vacant flats confirmed this supposition. On the other hand, unsatisfied demand for low-rent housing had continued. If the industry were now to concentrate on this line, there would be almost unlimited opportunities for many years to come. At the moment, the provision of low-rent accommodation is mainly the responsibility of the Government within the resettlement plans. Some industrial enterprises, especially textile factories, provide dormitories for their workers. Co-operative building societies are encouraged, but so far this movement has been very limited. Apart from government construction of schools, hospitals,

---

[1] Moreover, export of locally produced cement was regarded as more profitable than sales in the home market.

offices, stadiums, piers, sea-walls, roads, water reservoirs, the airfield, bridges, and reclamation of land, &c., mention should also be made of considerable constructional work carried out for the British forces stationed in the New Territories. Privately financed community projects, including medical, educational, and recreational facilities, also provide an important contribution to the growth of the Colony's building and construction industry.

DERIVED DEMAND FOR NON-METALLIC AND CHEMICAL PRODUCTS

Non-metallic Products

Closely linked with building and construction was the expansion of the manufacture of cement and allied non-metallic products. Local production of cement is undertaken by the Green Island Cement Co. The Company suffered severely during the occupation, and half of its machinery was removed by the Japanese. This has all been replaced from the United Kingdom, so that the Company's present manufacturing capacity is now exceeding the pre-war level of 100,000 tons p.a.

The manufacture of cement is an expensive process, as few of the raw materials required for its manufacture are found locally, except clay and iron ore. Limestone has to be imported from Indochina, China, or Japan; coal from Japan, China, Indochina, Indonesia, India, or even farther afield; gypsum from America or the Mediterranean countries; and paper bags principally from Europe. In spite of this, thanks to the cheap labour force consisting of 260 persons, the Company was able to compete not only in the local market but also abroad by exporting from one-third to two-thirds of its annual output. The works of the Company are situated on the water-front and, as it possesses its own fleet of lighters, it is well equipped to handle export business. By 1956 the quantity exported increased to 123,690 tons and the value to HK$7·9 million, with North Borneo as the main buyer (HK$3·8 million), followed by Malaya (HK$2 million) and South Korea (HK$1·3 million).

There are two factories producing bricks, and one plant producing tiles and blocks. Their whole output is sold locally. The same applies to pottery, glass, gypsum, plaster articles, abrasives, and lime. The whole non-metallic-products industry consisted of 61 undertakings in 1954. By 1956 this number increased to 73, and employment from 2,171 to 2,379.[1]

Paints

Another line of manufacture closely associated with the post-war housing boom was the production of paints and lacquers, part of Hong Kong's chemical industry. In 1947 the Colony's chemical industry comprised only 42 factories with 2,217 employees. By 1955 the number of factories increased to 90 and employment to 3,144. Table 36 (p. 172) shows the structure of this industry in March 1955.

Before the Second World War paint production in Hong Kong was economically insignificant and was confined to simple oleo-resinous general-purpose paints and quick-drying enamels, mainly suitable for interior applications. There were only four small factories engaged in producing low-grade paint, mostly for local consumers of lower-bracket incomes. After the war, Hong Kong embarked upon a large reconstruction and building programme, and as in the immediate post-war years good-quality imported paints were very short in supply, building contractors turned to local paints. By 1956 the number of paint factories increased to 10, employing altogether 471 workers. Most factories are highly mechanized and equipped with the latest types of machinery. Most of the raw materials are imported from the United Kingdom, and smaller amounts from the United States, Belgium, Sweden, Denmark, Western Germany, and South Africa. Some essential oils (linseed, tung oil, &c.) and resins are also imported from China. Constant research and laboratory tests serve to improve the quality of products until they are able to withstand subtropical climatic conditions and can compare favourably with any of the imported brands. The most important recent advance was the development of emulsion paints.

The industry produces annually some 11,000 tons of various types of paint, worth about HK$22 million, 60 per cent. of which is exported. The largest single local buyer is the Public Works Department. Other buyers are: shipping, shipbuilding and ship repairing, transport companies, the building industry,

[1] *Hong Kong Annual Report 1956*, p. 302.

repairs and maintenance contractors, &c. The total local consumption is estimated at about 5,000 tons p.a., of which only about 1,000 tons is supplied by imported brands, i.e. 80 per cent. of all local needs is met by the local factories and a substantial export trade is being built up. Malaya, Thailand, Burma, North Borneo, and the Philippines are the biggest importers.

Cosmetics

Unlike paints and lacquers, the manufacture of cosmetics—another branch of the Colony's chemical industry—has not expanded greatly since the war. There were several causes for this, the most important being the loss of the Chinese market. At the turn of the century, cosmetic articles began to be made in Hong Kong by a small firm which, after a few years, developed into a large manufacturing concern. Between 1910 and 1925 several new companies were established. The industry was reaching its zenith when China gained tariff autonomy in 1928, and the greater part of the exports of cosmetics from Hong Kong to China was lost. But other foreign markets, especially Malaya and the Dutch East Indies, were retained. Following the establishment of the Communist régime, the mainland market for cosmetics, regarded as 'luxury' goods, had to be completely abandoned. The increased home demand became the main source of orders, but overseas markets in Malaya, Indonesia, North Borneo, and Guam Island were also regained and expanded. Total value of output of the industry can be estimated at HK$4 million p.a., 60 per cent. of which is destined for export.

At the end of 1956 the 10 registered factories producing cosmetics employed 257 workers (207 in 1948), 40 per cent. of whom were women. Only small-size machines are used for heating, stirring, and bottling; finishing and packing is normally done by hand. Most of the raw materials are imported from the United Kingdom and France, and smaller amounts from the Netherlands, Switzerland, the United States, and China. So far, only the most common varieties of cosmetics (colognes, Florida water, perfumed soaps, face creams and powders, toilet and baby powders, hair oils and creams, tooth pastes and powders) have been produced. Local consumption of foreign cosmetics in 1955 amounted to HK$13·7 million. There is, therefore, scope for expansion of this industry, even if only for the local market.

One of the reasons explaining the difficulties in competing with foreign products is the fact that cosmetics are subject to customs and excise duty. This was equal to 10 per cent. of the retail price, irrespective of the country of origin, until December 1947, when it was raised to 25 per cent. on the selling price ex-factory for locally manufactured cosmetics, and on the f.o.b. price ex-shipping port for imported cosmetics. As a result of this change, retail prices of locally produced cosmetics went up by 11·5 per cent. whereas retail prices of imported cosmetics rose by only 9 per cent. Manufacturers thus complain that the 1947 change in the system of taxation of cosmetics has produced a great handicap to this industry. It seems that the reduction of the duty could provide a stimulus to its development.

Matches

Another branch of the chemical industry which not only did not expand but even began to contract is the production of matches. This is about twenty years old, although some domestic manufacture began earlier. Only 3 factories have survived up to 1956, and all domestic match-making has disappeared. In March 1947 these 3 factories employed 985 workers. At the end of 1956 the total labour force declined to 568, about three-quarters being women. Even with its low level of wages, the Hong Kong match industry cannot compete with Macao, where workers are paid less. This, and the simplicity of the process of manufacture, enabled Macao to develop the match industry into one of its main lines of export. For the same reasons, Macao also surpassed Hong Kong in the production of firecrackers, joss sticks, and mosquito sticks.[1] As a result, about 50 per cent. of the demand for matches in Hong Kong is being met by imports from Macao, local manufacturers sharing the remaining half of the market.

In these circumstances the two larger match factories turned their attention to overseas markets, particularly in the Com-

---

[1] The yearly estimated average export value of these main industries of Macao is as follows: matches HK$2 million, fire-crackers HK$4 million, incense sticks HK$0·6 million.

monwealth countries where they could enjoy the benefits of imperial preference. In connexion with this, most of the chemical raw materials were imported from Britain, and timber from Canada. Exports were developed to the value of over HK$2 million in 1954 and 1955. More than 50 per cent. of this was sold in Malaya, 30 per cent. in Indonesia, and the rest in Africa, the Philippines, and Australia, New Zealand, and other Commonwealth countries. In 1956 there was a heavy decline in the value of these exports. One of the reasons was the closure of the Suez Canal, which greatly increased the cost of raw materials imported from Britain and Canada so that the industry had to import timber and also other materials from Japan and China. China herself became a strong competitor in Malaya and Indonesia, and even in the Hong Kong home market. In some countries, especially in Africa and Pakistan, local production was developed. Finally, the increase in the Malayan tariff in September 1956 produced a decrease of Hong Kong exports of matches to Malaya to 20 per cent. of the 1955 level. As a result, the total value of exports declined to HK$0·7 million in 1956. Had it not been for the substantial increase in the volume of exports to the Philippines, the Hong Kong manufacture of matches would be almost at a standstill.

It is not likely that this industry will ever expand in Hong Kong to a more significant extent. The manufacture of matches may be regarded as an instance of an industry which will have to wither in the course of economic growth. Countries which are at a lower stage of economic development will take it over, and the Colony's labour and capital resources will be shifted one stage upwards. This is, in a sense, an inevitable law of economic development.

COMPLEMENTARY DEMAND FOR FURNITURE, METAL PRODUCTS, AND ELECTRICAL APPARATUS

Furniture

The impact of Hong Kong's housing boom on the manufacture of wood and rattan furniture and fixtures was pronounced. In 1947 this industry comprised 25 recorded and registered factories with 602 employees. By 1956 the number of factories increased to 131 and employment to 2,214. No data are available as to the number of workers in non-recorded factories, but total employment may well exceed 5,000. The importance of derived demand for iron, copper, paint, nails, and so on should also be stressed. Apart from satisfying local demand, this industry has been working for export.

Chinese art-carved teakwood and camphorwood chests and boxes have long been world famous, but before the Second World War their manufacture was chiefly concentrated in Shanghai and Canton. Only two or three small firms existed in Hong Kong. There were, however, many firms producing rosewood, blackwood, and well seasoned wood furniture for local consumption. After the war, with the increase in house construction, the output of this furniture was greatly stimulated. Simultaneously, manufacturing of art-carved teakwood chests developed, mainly for export. In 1956 the total value of exported wooden furniture exceeded HK$9 million. Most of this consisted of art-carved teakwood chests, and 90 per cent. of exports went to the United States and Panama, the rest to the United Kingdom.

The manufacture of rattan furniture was started in Hong Kong in 1916. Almost from the beginning, production for export developed, and this was resumed and expanded after the Second World War. Most of the raw materials are imported from Malaya and Java, and smaller amounts from Burma, North Borneo, and the Philippines. There are no data concerning the value of output and exports in this branch. Comparing it, however, with the wooden furniture, and, considering that up to 95 per cent. of output is exported, the value of exports of rattan furniture could be estimated at certainly no less than HK$10 million p.a. About 90 per cent. of this was sent to the United States, the remainder to the United Kingdom, Australia, Western Germany, and New Zealand. Technical progress and a widening of the variety of products, if combined with marketing improvements, may result in further expansion of this prosperous industry.

Metal Products

Another sector stimulated by derived demand originating from construction and building, and by complementary demand for house equipment, was the manufacture of various metal products. From very modest beginnings, such as the manufacture of nails and screws, this industry has grown in the course of about fifty years into one of the biggest sources of employment, and is still expanding. In 1947 it included 88 factories with 4,365 workers. By 1955 the number of factories increased to 336 and the number of employees to 15,756. Its products, furthermore, were more varied, including over fifty items which can be divided into the following main groups: (1) products used for the construction of houses; (2) intermediate products for other industries; (3) household goods; (4) military equipment; and (5) other miscellaneous metal products developed as side-lines. A more detailed picture is given in Table 37 (p. 173).

Diversification in this industry is remarkable. Production of all these goods requires raw materials which have to be imported, and considerable ingenuity has been shown in finding them, especially scrap. Many factories have been buying wrecked vessels as scrap, out of which reinforcing bars for buildings and for other purposes were produced. Black-plate wasters for the production of enamelware were imported mainly from the United States and the United Kingdom. Scrap from brass and steel cartridge-cases and other military equipment was bought in Okinawa, the Philippines, and other battlefields of the Second World War. This scrap was then re-rolled or re-melted for various uses, such as making brass strips for electric-torch cases.

Enamelware

The history of the enamelware industry provides the most typical pattern of growth. The industry was started in 1932, following the example of Shanghai. The methods of manufacture were copied from Japan. The first factory (Keung Wah Aluminium & Enamelware Factory), which was founded by a group of overseas Chinese from America, was not very successful, and in 1937 it was sold to the I-Feng Enamelling Co., which has since remained the leading enterprise. In 1938 another enamelware factory was established, the Dai Ward Steel Works, which was removed from Canton after this city had been occupied by the Japanese. The products, because of their fine quality and competitive prices, immediately began

H

to attract the attention of overseas buyers, and demand was growing until 1941, when the war brought the industry to a standstill. Its rapid expansion after the war was one of the outstanding features of the Colony's industrial development. As mentioned, Shanghai was more advanced than Hong Kong in this field. It possessed many first-class entrepreneurs with large capital resources. When Shanghai was taken over by the Communists, many of these industrialists found refuge in Hong Kong, where they almost immediately entered this field of manufacture, which was familiar to them.

The industry did not require highly skilled labour, and the situation in world markets was favourable owing to the absence of Japanese competition and the closure of many markets for goods produced in China. Moreover, many other producing countries were trying to meet their home requirements first, and left unsatisfied a large demand in the South Seas, Africa, and the Middle East. Hong Kong manufacturers were quick to seize this opportunity and rapid development followed. From 2 factories with 6 furnaces before the war, the industry grew to 39 factories operating 90 furnaces in 1956, and employment increased to 6,157 which constituted 4·3 per cent. of all workers employed in recorded and registered factories. To this, employment in unregistered enterprises should be added. The value of exports in 1956 exceeded HK$76 million, i.e. about 10 per cent. of the total export value of locally manufactured goods.

Most of the raw materials are supplied by the United States, the United Kingdom, and Canada. Only the initial processes (blanking, drawing, trimming, and wiring) are mechanized. On the whole, the plant is not up to date; much of it is second hand, brought earlier from the mainland factories, but there is plenty of ingenuity, and a number of original machines, built locally to the design of individual factories, are in operation. Of the total annual output of about HK$90 million, less than 14 per cent. is sold locally, the rest being exported. The principal markets include Africa, Malaya, Indonesia, the British West Indies, Central and South America, Ceylon, and the Philippines. Few manufacturers handle exports themselves, so that overseas trade is mostly in the hands of local exporters. Joint efforts of the manufacturers, organized in the Enamelware

Manufacturers' Association, enabled them to compete with Japanese and Czechoslovak exporters by standardizing prices and co-ordinating sales policies.[1]

As mentioned before, the development of the enamelware industry presents a pattern which applies to several other branches of the metal-products industry, especially metal lanterns, vacuum flasks, aluminium ware, and tin cans. These lines of manufacture have contributed considerably to the recent increase in the value of exports of Hong Kong manufactured products.

Electro-plating

In the order of employment figures, electro-plating in 1955–6 reached third place among the branches of the metal-products industry, after enamelware and tin-can manufacture. It was established in the Colony before the Second World War, when the most common platings employed were gold, silver, and nickel. Nickel plating, which served for most of the commercial purposes, consisted chiefly of dull plating, and the labour involved in polishing this raised costs so much that the whole industry became economically unimportant.

However, the growth of numerous branches of the metal-products industry after the war encouraged a large number of people to engage in electro-plating. Technical progress presented the second favourable factor, for the introduction of bright nickel plating created a larger profit margin. Thirdly, in recent years, decreasing costs of raw materials enabled copper, tin, chromium, and zinc plating to become gradually commercialized. As a result, until a few years ago, profits were calculated in this industry at 250–300 per cent. These attractive margins caused a rapid growth of electro-plating establishments, especially as only limited technical knowledge and relatively little capital were required. Thus from 5 firms in 1947 the industry grew to 51 in 1956 and employment increased from 287 to 1,134. These figures refer only to registered and recorded factories. However, it was estimated in 1956 that more than 300 enterprises were actually operating, some being no more than family workshops. At least 2,000 persons, therefore, were

[1] On the whole, the co-ordinating activity of this Association has been a failure.

probably employed in this industry in 1956. Multiplication of firms has reduced profit margins to about 50 per cent. of the revenue, cost of labour forming 40 per cent. of the total, and raw materials the remaining 10 per cent.

Most of the raw materials are imported from Western Germany, the United Kingdom, and the United States, and smaller amounts from Japan. The processes of electro-plating have not yet been fully mechanized. The high capital cost, the relative inflexibility in comparison with a manual-plating installation, and the high maintenance charges do not make it worth while to use the fully-automatic plating machines. The industry is not working directly for export. Its contribution is indirect by providing a 'finishing' touch to a number of locally manufactured products. Gold plating is thus used in the production of watch bands, badges, medals, brooches, and cigarette cases. Silver plating is used for choppers, knives, ash trays, locks, kitchen utensils, and surgical instruments. Zinc plating is employed in the production of steel wire, the chassis of radio sets, telephone equipment, electronic apparatus and steel conduit piping. Copper, nickel, and chromium platings are used for electric torches, tops and bottoms of vacuum flasks, metal-working tools, and motor-car and tram-car accessories, such as bumpers, and bars. Some tin plating is employed in the production of tin cans. The most important application of electro-plating is in the production of electrical machinery, apparatus, and appliances, especially in the manufacture of electric torches.

Electrical Apparatus

None of the Hong Kong metal products, except enamelware, has achieved the significance of the industry producing electric torches, bulbs, and batteries, which together contributed over 9 per cent. to the total value of exports of Hong Kong products in 1955. The first enterprise in this line, the Nam Jam Factory, was established in 1928; two years later the Sunbeam Manufacturing Co. started, and a number of other factories followed. After the war a new expansionary phase began and the industry rapidly gained a world-wide reputation, as, from the very beginning, efforts were made to produce chiefly for foreign markets. The number of factories producing torches, bulbs, and batteries increased from 36 in 1946 to 70 in 1955, and employment grew from 2,269 to 8,075, of whom about 75 per cent. are women.

The raw materials for torches, consisting chiefly of brass, aluminium, tin-plate, and plastics, are mostly imported from the United Kingdom, United States, Western Germany, and Japan. The large content of British raw materials enabled the industry to make full use of the benefits resulting from imperial preference, but Hong Kong torches are exported to almost all countries of the world. In 1956 the United States accounted for about 13 per cent. of the total value of this export. Two large American concerns, Ever-ready and Ray-O-Vac, obtain torches from the Colony by regular contracts with the factories which are licensed and financed by them.

Usually torches are exported together with bulbs and batteries, but the two latter products are also sold independently. The torchlight dry cells with the trade mark Five Rams had already become known all over the world before the Second World War. The home market takes only about 10 per cent. of output. In 1955 the export of batteries exceeded HK$10 million (over 60 million batteries), the bulk of which was sent to Indonesia, Malaya, Indochina, Thailand, and African countries. The value of exports of torch bulbs in 1955 was almost HK$6 million (over 10 million dozen), India being the chief customer.

Besides torches, batteries, and bulbs, the Hong Kong electrical industry is now producing a wide range of electrical appliances, such as electric clocks, fans, fires, irons, kettles, and radio and telephone condensers. The production of electric clocks initiated by Chiap Hua Manufactory Co. in 1953 marked the beginning of Hong Kong's precision-engineering industry, which has good prospects for further development. In 1955 there were 3 factories producing various electrical appliances and employing 111 workers. Another 3 factories were supplying neon lighting, and there were 2 registered radio-repairing workshops with 183 employees. Thus the total employment in 1955, in 78 registered establishments producing electrical machinery, apparatus, and appliances, amounted to 8,384 persons. This constituted 7·07 per cent. of the total number of workers in registered and recorded factories, so that the electrical industry was fourth in the order of employment among all manufacturing industries in the Colony (after textiles, metal products, and transport equipment). The total value of output of this industry in 1955 amounted to about HK$75 million.

FURTHER CUMULATIVE EFFECTS: THE GROWTH OF THE MACHINE INDUSTRY

The growth of industries such as building and construction, furniture, chemical, metal, and electrical products, as well as textiles and plastics, gave rise to the development of the Colony's machine industry. All industries need some kind of machinery, or at least spare parts and repair services, and reliance on foreign machine industry is not only costly but time-consuming. These were the main reasons why Hong Kong developed the production of diesel engines for generating sets, vehicles, vessels, and pumps; water pumps; guillotines; engine lathes; manual presses; drilling, milling, knitting, spinning, weaving, and shaping machines; machinery for enamelware and can-making factories; machinery for electrical industry, &c.

Before the war this industry was very small. It was chiefly connected with the manufacture of various metal products. Other industries relied mainly on foreign machines. The leading role in the development of the local machine industry was played by the Chiap Hua Manufactory, which was founded in 1937 to produce various types of metal articles. In 1939 two aluminium-manufacturing factories were established, the Wah Chong Metal Works and the Ting Tai Metal Works, which also began to produce some machinery. Between 1938 and 1941 several metal-products enterprises switched to the manufacture of small machinery and parts to meet the demand of various new factories. The Japanese occupation, however, resulted in the almost complete ruin of this industry.

After the war, scarcity of raw materials and capital goods brought about great difficulties in the reconstruction of Hong Kong's machine industry, but the pressure of local demand was sufficiently powerful to overcome these obstacles. Influx of capital and entrepreneurial skill from China played its usual role, so that several new large machine-manufacturing companies were formed, equipment was secured from abroad, and the industry began to operate and expand. Apart from machine manufacture, there emerged a large number of machine-

repairing establishments. The number of registered and recorded firms in the Colony's machine industry amounted to 155
in 1955. This should be compared with 54 establishments which
employed 967 workers in March 1947. In 1955 employment
amounted to about 2,300 workers, 96 per cent. of whom were
men. The degree of mechanization in the industry is fairly high.
Electricity is the source of energy, and some larger firms have
their own generators. Almost all raw materials (steel, tin, iron,
zinc, and alloy minerals) have to be imported, chiefly from the
United States, Indonesia, and Malaya. The annual output is
estimated at approximately HK$75 million. Production is
mainly for the home market but a small part of it is exported,
e.g. some printing machines, plastic presses, and machines for
making glass are sent to Malaya, the Philippines, and Indonesia. It is very likely that these exports will gradually increase,
for Hong Kong machines are simple and easily adjustable to
various needs; repairs require little ingenuity, and spare parts
for them can be produced in almost any country.

9

The Expansion of Clothing and Food Manufacture

NEXT to the housing and construction boom, the increase in the demand for clothing was the second main driving force in Hong Kong's industrial expansion. In 1956 the textile industry gave employment to 42,254 workers in registered and recorded factories alone. This figure should be at least doubled to obtain the figure of total employment. The industry absorbed one-third of the total labour force engaged in the recorded and registered establishments, and its output formed about 60 per cent. of the total value of exports of Hong Kong manufactured goods. It now covers all processes, i.e. rope-making; spinning, weaving, knitting, dyeing, finishing, and printing of cotton, silk, rayon, and wool; and also includes the manufacture of made-up garments such as shirts, pyjamas, and underwear.

The earliest branch of this industry, rope-making, was established some seventy years ago in conjunction with the fishing industry. The most important factory is now the Hongkong Rope Manufacturing Co., with a monthly output of 2 million lb. of rope. Besides this factory, there are 42 registered rope-manufacturing establishments which employ about 900 workers. Another old branch of Hong Kong's textile industry is weaving and knitting, which began long ago with machines entirely worked by hand, operating in tenement buildings and in cottage back rooms. This produced, for the most part, fabrics for domestic purposes within the family. The power looms which were later installed to produce fabrics on a commercial scale did not entirely replace the hand looms. This branch of the textile industry steadily expanded, especially in the thirties under the influence of imperial preference, so that before the Second World War its output was estimated at about 80 million yards a year, most of which was sold abroad. On the whole, however, the manufacture of textiles was of minor importance in the years before 1941. Since 1945 the industry has greatly expanded. Manufacture of all pre-war items has been revived, and an important cotton and wool spinning section and modern weaving sheds have been added. Recent additions to the industry are woollen gloves, nylon knitting, and the manufacture of carpets.

The year 1947 opened a new era in the annals of Hong Kong's industries, when the South China Textile Co. made its debut. Development has been phenomenally rapid. By 1950 the production of cotton yarns had grown sufficiently in volume to provide fully for local weaving and knitting needs and still leave a surplus for export. The number of cotton-spinning mills increased to 13 in 1951, and to 19 in 1956. In 1956 they employed over 14,000 workers and operated approximately 300,000 spindles, consuming about 250,000 bales of cotton. Table 38 (p. 174) gives a more detailed picture of this industry in 1955.

Most of Hong Kong's cotton mills were established between 1948 and 1950, when, in view of the political events on the mainland, many Chinese entrepreneurs decided to spread their investments. As part of this policy, they diverted to Hong Kong shipments of textile machinery already ordered, or purchased additional quantities of textile equipment to be delivered to Hong Kong.

With the change of regime in China in 1949, many workers from Swatow, a place noted for embroidery, moved to Hong Kong; and it was their skill and experience in needlework which helped to expand this industry locally. There are now over 30 registered embroidery establishments.

The manufacture of Hong Kong *kikoy* (a sarong-like garment) came into being in 1948. This industry was in the hands of Japanese weavers before the Second World War. In 1947 an African merchant succeeded in arousing the interest of the Ng Yee Hing Co. When orders became too large for one factory the buyers sought other weavers, and thus a new branch of Hong Kong's weaving industry was born. There are now about 150 registered weaving factories (including 8 large ones), employing together over 9,000 workers.

The woollen-glove industry is one of the latest and most modern additions. Only a few years ago, the knitted-woollen-glove markets in America and Europe were almost monopolized by Japan. Early in 1952 Hong Kong exporters, in co-operation with some small knitting works in Kowloon, succeeded in introducing the locally knitted woollen gloves to European markets. The result was so encouraging that this particular branch of the industry is now flourishing. Hong Kong woollen gloves are fast replacing Japanese goods in Europe. One of the biggest glove-knitting factories in the Colony is the Oriental Corporation, which not only knits gloves but also spins its own yarn. In 1956 there were 3 wool-spinning mills in Hong Kong; they employed 847 workers. The knitting industry as a whole consisted in 1956 of 325 registered establishments employing over 14,000 workers. There are 8 registered factories engaged solely in the manufacture of woollen gloves, but other registered knitting mills also undertake this work in addition to the manufacture of other types of knitwear.

Raw cotton is imported into the Colony from various parts of the world: the United States, Pakistan, India, Burma, Egypt, Turkey, Brazil, Mexico, Iran, Syria, and East Africa. The woollen-glove industry depends principally (80 per cent.) upon the supply of wool tops and woollen yarn imported from the United Kingdom. But Japan supplies 66 per cent. of the Colony's woollen yarn as compared with 25 per cent. from the United Kingdom, although it is probable that Japanese yarn is spun from imported (mainly Australian) wool. For the embroidery factories some locally woven cotton cloth is used, mainly for linen bags and pillow-cases; most of the cloth, however, is imported. Nylon for blouses and underwear is imported from America and the United Kingdom. High-grade linen and cotton from Switzerland, and from Northern Ireland and other parts of the United Kingdom are used for table-cloths, mats, luncheon sets, and finely embroidered handkerchiefs. Artificial silk of Japanese origin is also used.

Table 39 (p. 175) gives the number of factories and persons employed in each section of the Colony's textile industry in 1955. Machinery in the spinning mills is for the greater part as up to date and as efficient as can be found anywhere in the world, and housed in modern factory buildings. Some mills are also equipped for weaving, for which they utilize the latest type of automatic looms. The equipment of the smaller and older weaving and knitting factories is, however, capable of improvement. The weaving factories operate some 4,000 power looms besides a considerable number of hand looms. Recently one of the spinning mills acquired a modern unit for the pressure dyeing of yarns in packages. Some big factories have been equipped with carding and combing machines, drying chambers for drying the dyed yarns, and self-packing machines.

The Hong Kong textile industry is leaving its mark on world markets. Its total export value is in the vicinity of HK$500 million p.a. Of the total output of cotton yarn, between 40 and 50 per cent. is taken up by local weaving and knitting mills, the balance being exported to Indonesia, Indochina, Thailand, the United Kingdom, South Korea, Burma, the Philippines, and Pakistan. Minor quantities find their way into the Australian and African markets. Cloth (sheetings, shirtings, drills, mats, osnaburgs, cellular fabrics, checks, suitings, and silk brocades), tapes, webbing, laces, &c. are exported mainly to the United Kingdom, Indonesia, Malaya, Thailand, Africa, the Philippines, Australia, South Korea, Indochina, Macao, the West Indies and the United States. Printed cloth is now well received in Africa, as well as in North Borneo and the Philippines.

Most of the cotton singlets are sent to Malaya, Indonesia, Thailand, Macao, and Africa. The greatest export of towels is to the United Kingdom, Thailand, Malaya, and the West Indies. There is a large demand for Hong Kong embroidered goods in Central and South America, Japan, New Zealand, and Australia. The industry also includes sizeable garment manufacture, hat making, and the distribution of men's suits by mail order. By far the greatest part of the export of Hong Kong gloves [1] of all kinds is sent to the United Kingdom. The United States, Canada, Australia, and New Zealand also take considerable quantities.

In spite of its considerable success, the future of Hong Kong's textile industry is very uncertain. Many of the importing countries have recently become politically independent. Some have been the scene of social troubles and have not yet found

[1] See Table 40, p. 176.

real stability, but others have industrialized to such an extent that they have become exporting countries. The trend in all of them is to become self-sufficient, and exports to such countries must decline. On the other hand, increasing populations and a general rise in the standard of living may contribute to sustaining the present level of textile exports from Hong Kong.

FOOTWEAR MANUFACTURE

Rubber Industry

The manufacture of rubber products gives employment to over 6 per cent. of the total registered labour force in Hong Kong, being the fifth on the list of the Colony's industries. With over seventy factories in 1956, this industry includes not only rubber footwear, which is the main product, but also baby comforters and bottle teats, sheetings, hose-pipes, balls, toys, dolls and balloons, bicycle tyres and tubes, elastic bands, erasers, rubber stamps, and underwater swimming wear. The changing fortunes of this industry are very typical of the Colony's economic development.

The manufacture of rubber goods is one of Hong Kong's oldest industries. It began over thirty years ago when two small factories were established mainly for the manufacture of rubber soles and heels and also, to a lesser extent, for the production of shoes for the local market. In 1926 several new factories were opened and the goods began to be sold in China, export amounting to 1 million pairs of rubber shoes a year. This should be compared with the position in 1955, when the total export amounted to about 4·5 million pairs, not counting canvas shoes with rubber soles and other products of this industry. Development gained momentum when merchants established contact with buyers much farther afield. There were many difficulties and setbacks, but the turning point occurred in 1932, when an order came for a shipment to the British West Indies. Because of the reasonable price and good quality of the merchandise, the demand soon became large enough to justify the establishment of more factories. In the course of time the United Kingdom became the chief market.

After the war quick recovery took place, and, from 1947 onwards, orders for the local market continued to be steady.

In the absence of foreign demand for footwear, factories were compensated to some extent by orders for other rubber products, chiefly bicycle tyres and tubes for nearby markets. In August 1947 an order for approximately 2½ million pairs of rubber shoes was received from the United Kingdom. In 1949 Hong Kong rubber footwear was placed on the open General Licence in the United Kingdom. The years 1950–1 were the peak period of the industry. New difficulties appeared with the outbreak of hostilities in Korea, when manufacturers were faced continuously with the burden of the rising cost of their basic raw materials. The flourishing export to China came to an abrupt stop with the imposition of the embargo on the export of rubber manufactures (chiefly raw rubber and tyres for vehicles). However, during the last few years, more orders were received from the United Kingdom, Canada, and other Commonwealth countries, so that the number of factories has increased from 51 in 1952 to 72 (with 7,386 workers) in 1956.

About 70 per cent. of the labour force are women. All rubber is imported from Malaya and North Borneo, and carbon black from the United States. Canvas is still imported from the United Kingdom, but locally made canvas is increasingly used, as well as drills for lining, and millions of eyelets and laces.

The main countries importing rubber footwear from the Colony in 1955 were: the United Kingdom (78 per cent.), Africa (6 per cent.), Canada (5·6 per cent.). Minor quantities were exported to Australia, Western Germany, the British West Indies, South America, &c. Canvas shoes with rubber soles were exported chiefly to the United Kingdom (63 per cent.), Canada (17 per cent.), Africa (6 per cent.), Belgium (3 per cent.), Netherlands (2 per cent.), Western Germany (1·3 per cent), smaller quantities being sent to Australia, Central America, Burma, and other countries. The value of exports of these two items constituted about 8 per cent. of the total value of exports of Hong Kong manufactured goods in 1955. The Association of Hongkong Rubber Footwear Manufacturers keeps an eye on the quality of the footwear and works together with the Hongkong Rubber Footwear Exporters Association. These Associations were founded early in 1941, mainly to regulate war-time trade.

Leather Industry

A substantial supply of footwear for local consumption and for export has been provided by Hong Kong's leather industry. The industry also includes the production of leather bags, belts, footballs, photograph frames, purses, suit-cases, trunks, gloves, and watch straps. All the leather-manufacturing enterprises in Hong Kong are run by Chinese owners, many of whom are immigrants from Shanghai. Besides a large number of small enterprises, there were in 1956 fifteen major tanneries and leather factories. Table 41 (p. 176) indicates the growth of this industry from 1947 to 1955 as illustrated by the number of registered factories and of employees working in them.

The main sources of supply of raw hides and leather are China, Indochina, Thailand, Malaya, Australia, and Canada. Hong Kong itself also produces a small amount of raw hides, but they are only used for Chinese slippers or cheaper shoes. Until recently, the industry was employing only obsolete methods of production. A few years ago, however, modern methods of manufacturing were introduced and suitable machines were imported from the United Kingdom and Denmark.

In 1955 the total value of exports of leather shoes produced in the Colony amounted to HK$14·2 million. Of 1·2 million pairs exported, 50 per cent. was sent to Malaya, 13 per cent. to United States Oceania, 10 per cent. to Thailand, 7 per cent. to Africa, and 5 per cent. to the British West Indies. Other leather goods manufactured in Hong Kong are exported to the Philippines, Singapore, South America, &c. A large number of belts are sent to Indonesia, and substantial quantities of military shoes are exported to Thailand. Neither leather nor leather goods can now find a market in China, where, in order to protect the local industry, very high import duties are imposed.

FOOD, BEVERAGES, AND TOBACCO MANUFACTURE

Food

Unlike many newly born Hong Kong industries, food manufacturing is mostly undertaken by local people, and consequently is not so much influenced by the influx of the northern industrialists. The number of workers engaged in 1956 in 323 registered establishments in the food-manufacturing industry was 6,708, constituting over 5 per cent. of the total registered labour force. Most of the products of this industry are locally consumed, but canned goods, preserved ginger, and other foodstuffs, as well as sugar, are exported.

Long before the Second World War, canned goods from Hong Kong used to be exported to all parts of the world: the United States, Malaya, the Netherlands, East and West Africa, &c. During the war this export ceased, but after the end of the war the accumulated demand, especially that of the Chinese overseas, revived the industry, which began to prosper again.

Among 78 canning factories registered in 1955, the Amoy Canning Corporation was the most outstanding. It was the first factory in China to can goods in cans made on the premises. About thirty years ago the Company moved from Amoy to Hong Kong and built canning and soya-sauce bottling plants there. It now also includes an oil refinery (started in 1951), a bean-cake plant, and facilities for the preserving of many other delicacies. The foodstuffs used for canning are fish, meat, fruits, vegetables, poultry, and soya beans. The tin-plate for can-making is imported from England, while other materials are either local products or imported from China. The factory in Hong Kong, employing about 500 workers, is only one of four branches of the Company, three of which were at Amoy, Canton, and Shanghai. When the Communists took over China, these branches were closed down, but a new factory was established in Singapore and another one in Kuala Lumpur. The Company has the most modern can-making equipment and turns out cans at the rate of 200 a minute. Canned foods and soya sauces are sent to various places in South East Asia. About 80 per cent. of the Amoy Company's lychees are exported to the United Kingdom.

In 1955 the value of exports of all locally preserved fruit amounted to HK$13·4 million, of which 52 per cent. was sent to Malaya, 24 per cent. to the United States, 5 per cent. to Burma, 3 per cent. to North Borneo, and smaller quantities to Indochina, the Philippines, Indonesia, the United Kingdom, the British West Indies, Australia, and others.

About 120 years ago in Canton, a hawker named Li Chy

first conceived the idea of preserving ginger in syrup. His formula, though simple, opened up vast commercial possibilities. Li Chy subsequently changed the name of his factory to Chy Loong Ginger Factory, and in 1845 removed it to Hong Kong. His success soon attracted other investors, so that by 1915 there were eleven independent factories. In 1937 some members of the trade formed a syndicate (Hongkong Preserved Ginger Distributors) in order to develop new confections, improve packing, open up new markets, and stabilize prices. As a result, in 1939 about 6½ million lb. of preserved ginger were exported, chiefly to Europe, the United States, and Australia.

After the Second World War rehabilitation progressed rapidly, and in little more than a year exports of ginger were resumed, while the first post-war shipment to the United Kingdom was made in 1947. In spite of exchange restrictions imposed by various countries, the popularity of the product appeared to indicate a secure future until the introduction of the United Nations embargo, which meant that all ginger products were denied entry into the United States, since China had long been the traditional source of supply of raw ginger. However, the resources and enterprise of the syndicate kept the industry on a steady footing, at about HK$5 million annual export value. The volume of exports even increased from 2,200 tons in 1952 to 3,900 tons in 1955. The United Kingdom and the Netherlands are the main buyers. There are now eight ginger-preserving factories in Hong Kong, the largest belonging to the Amoy Canning Corporation.

Sugar refining in Hong Kong is carried out by the Taikoo Sugar Refining Company, established in 1884. It was rebuilt in 1926 and re-equipped with new machinery, making it the largest and most modern sugar refinery in the Far East. During the Second World War it suffered great damage, which necessitated considerable structural rehabilitation and ordering of new machinery, which began to arrive in 1950; refining was resumed in September of that year. The British Ministry of Food was then responsible for the supply of sugar to the nearby Colonial and Commonwealth area and, by arrangement with that Ministry, the requirements of Hong Kong, North Borneo, Sarawak, and Malaya were supplied either partly or in full by the Taikoo sugar refinery. When this arrangement ceased, ordinary commercial trading with these markets was restored. Most of the refined sugar is exported to Malaya, Singapore, North Borneo, Ceylon, Thailand, and South Africa. The annual output of the refinery is estimated at 50,000–60,000 tons, of which about 36,000 were exported each year during the 1954–6 period. The value of this export in 1955 was estimated at HK$24 million.[1]

Beverages

Both non-alcoholic and alcoholic beverages are produced in the Colony. The former type includes carbonated and non-carbonated drinks, while the latter can be divided into Chinese wine and beer. In 1956 there were 29 registered factories in the beverages industry, employing about 1,000 workers. The manufacture of soft drinks gave employment to over 50 per cent. of this number. The total annual output of the beverage industry in 1955 amounted to about HK$82 million (soft drinks HK$12 million, Chinese wine HK$50 million, beer HK$20 million). Most of the output is destined for local consumption, but the industry is exporting a small amount of non-alcoholic beverages and beer, mainly to North Borneo, Macao, Burma, Taiwan, and Indochina.

The manufacture of aerated water was first brought to China more than 150 years ago by the Dutch as one of the commodities for trade with the Netherlands, hence the popular term *Ho Loan Sui* or 'Holland Water'. In Hong Kong, from the early fifties of the last century, the name of Watson's has been connected with the manufacture of aerated waters. A. S. Watson & Co. was formally established in the Colony in 1867. Subsequently, it opened several branches in Shanghai, Foochow, Amoy, &c. As demand grew with the increase in population, a second factory producing aerated water, the Connaught Aerated Water Co., was opened in 1907. Prior to 1941 the total output of both companies amounted to about 1½ million dozen bottles a year. There are now 13 factories, producing about 4 million gallons of soft drinks a year and giving employment to approximately 600 workers. A duty of 48 cents per gallon is paid to the Government.

[1] The present author prepared in 1956 a detailed report on the Hong Kong Sugar Market, presented to *Banco Nacional de Cuba*.

I

The factories are of various sizes, and are using machinery which in some cases is antiquated and obsolete but in others quite up to date and efficient. The raw materials are obtained from various parts of the world. Orange juice, for example, is imported in tins from California; sugar is obtained either from the local market or imported from the Philippines, Taiwan, or Japan. The industry as a whole seems to have stabilized itself, and its future expansion is closely connected with the rate of population growth.

The growth of the Chinese wine industry was also rapid after the war. From 2 factories in 1949 this industry has grown to 15 in 1955; they gave employment to about 200 workers. Output amounts to about $1\frac{1}{4}$ million gallons a year and, as a duty of HK$6–7 per gallon is imposed, the Government derives over HK$7 million each year in the form of the wine tax. Two kinds of wine are produced: rice wine and medicinal wine. The former is made from rice combined mainly with sugar and soya bean. The latter possesses—so it is claimed—some nutritional, medicinal, and health-giving value. Production usually follows methods that date back to antiquity. Raw materials are imported, e.g. ginseng from South Korea, deer tail from New Zealand. Most of the wine produced is for local consumption, but there is some export to Singapore, Malaya, and Thailand.

The San Miguel Brewery, the only one in the Colony, was originally designed by the Skoda Works of Czechoslovakia, and in 1948 it was purchased by the present Company, which has its headquarters in Manila. The number of workers engaged in the production of beer increased from 156 in 1949 to 189 in 1955. The raw material for brewing is obtained from various countries: malt from the United Kingdom and Australia; hops from the United Kingdom and Germany. Tax is paid to the Government at the rate of HK$1·30 per gallon of beer produced in the brew-house. This is the only instance of preferential duty for a locally manufactured commodity. The beer produced is mainly for the local market, especially for the British forces. The future of this industry is thus closely connected with the number of British forces stationed in the Colony. There is a chance that local beer will gradually replace imported beer, because beer is now becoming more popular with the Chinese population, but no large expansion of this industry can be envisaged in the years to come.

Tobacco

In Hong Kong about 5 per cent. of an average family budget is spent on smoking, so that the total demand for various forms of tobacco may be estimated at about HK$90 million a year. Relatively high taxes are imposed on this outlay, and the tobacco duty amounted to about 10 per cent. of the total revenue of the Government during the 1949–54 period.[1] With tax amounting to HK$35 million and the value of retained imports of tobacco equal to HK$47 million, the net added value of the local tobacco industry can be estimated at around HK$8 million per annum. Thus it appears that the bulk of the Colony's demand for tobacco manufactures is satisfied by imports from abroad, but a fairly substantial contribution is made by the local tobacco industry.

While Chinese-type tobacco and inferior cigars are made in several small shops employing no machinery, there are several large factories. Two of them were established long before the Second World War, while the remaining three were organized after it. For a short time during the latter period British and American cigarettes were scarce. Taking advantage of these circumstances, the Nanyang Brothers Tobacco Co. and the British American Tobacco Co. used whatever raw materials were available and produced cigarettes to satisfy local demand. Other newly-established firms followed this lead, and output increased considerably between 1946 and 1949. From 1949 onwards the industry remained in a fairly stable equilibrium, with 6 factories employing about 1,300 workers in 1956.

Most of the workers employed are women and unskilled. Sorting and packing are done by hand, while, in the large factories, machinery is employed for the making of cigarettes and cigars. As no tobacco plants are cultivated in Hong Kong, raw materials are imported from the United States, Turkey, Egypt, the Philippines, and China. About 6 million lb. of tobacco leaf are imported into the Colony every year, 75 per cent. of which is of non-Empire origin. The industry manu-

---

[1] The present rate of duty on unmanufactured tobacco varies from HK$3·75 to 4·05 per lb (HK$3·55 to 3·85 for tobacco of Empire origin) and on manufactured tobacco (cigarettes and cigars) from HK$6·00 to 7·00 per lb (HK$4·50 to 4·70 for products of Empire origin and manufacture).

factures cigarettes and cigars of all qualities, including cheap Chinese-type tobacco. The bulk of the products is for local consumption. In 1955 the export value of locally manufactured cigarettes amounted to HK$683,256; most of them were sent to Macao (HK$606,285).

THE ICE AND COLD-STORAGE INDUSTRY

As Hong Kong is situated in the subtropical belt, the provision of cold-storage facilities and the manufacture of ice are essential for the preservation of foodstuffs and perishable goods. Compared with the other industries, the ice and cold-storage industry can hardly be called new, but it was only after the Second World War that it expanded.

The oldest existing firm in this industry is the Dairy Farm, Ice & Cold-Storage Co. Initially, it only provided dairy products. In 1915 the purchase of the only manufacturing ice company at that time, Hong Kong Ice Co., secured its leading position in the ice business. At about the same time, the operation of cold-storage facilities began. The quick expansion of this industry after the Second World War was primarily due to the rapidly increasing demand. Some local and Australian capitalists as well as refugees utilized their technological knowledge and capital to build up the industry to its present level, the high profit margin constituting the main attraction for investment. The number of firms increased from 4 before the war to 7 in 1951, and to 18 in 1955; whereas employment grew from 400 in 1951 to about 800 in 1955. During the peak period, which was around 1951, profits in the cold-storage industry ran as high as 150–200 per cent. of the operating costs. Now, the keen competition arising from the establishment of new firms and the decline in entrepôt trade have combined to reduce the profit margin only just to cover the cost of production and maintenance.

10

The Application of Inventions and the Effects of Cultural Progress

AMONG the industries of which no mention has yet been made, the following three main lines of development stand out:

1. First, a wide range of genuine 'new' industries which did not exist in Hong Kong before the war. Their development required either more imagination and enterprise or greater technical and artistic skill and precision than were formerly available. Examples are provided by the growth of the plastics industry, with its almost unlimited range of products; the manufacture of fountain pens, musical instruments, cameras, and gramophone records; or the development of the artificial-jewellery industry. The growth of all these industries provides a good illustration of the role of Rostowian propensities to apply science to economic ends and to accept innovations.[1] The name 'innovating industries' would not be inappropriate for this field of manufacture.

2. Secondly, the group of already existing industries which expanded in connexion with the cultural progress of the Colony, such as printing and publishing, and the related manufacture of paper; this category should also include the newly established Hong Kong film industry; the 'educational industry' consisting of numerous private schools of all types, from kindergartens to university colleges; and a number of cultural and artistic clubs and societies. The post-war cultural life of the Colony has been remarkably enriched, largely owing to the new social and intellectual group formed by the refugees from Mainland China and the increased interest in these matters being taken by the European element. These groups radically changed the pre-war 'mercantile', money-making character of Hong Kong, and introduced into it new educational, cultural, scientific, and artistic values.

[1] W. W. Rostow, *The Process of Economic Growth* (Oxford, Clarendon Press, 1953), p. 11.

3. Finally, a fairly wide and rapidly expanding range of enterprises producing tourists' goods and services: hotels, restaurants, night-clubs, cinemas, twenty-four-hours tailors, oriental souvenir shops, &c. This industry is rapidly becoming one of the most important income-generating sectors of the Colony's economy.

In the following pages an attempt will be made to characterize at least some of the major developments in these three fields of innovating, cultural, and tourist industries.

THE INNOVATING INDUSTRIES

Plastics

Hong Kong entrepreneurs quickly realized that the invention of plastics made possible the manufacture of an almost unlimited range of new commodities in the Colony, with its large, post-war reservoir of cheap labour. The plastics industry, which did not exist in Hong Kong before the war, is now one of the most firmly established. The pioneering firm was the Kader Industrial Co., which launched its manufacturing plan early in 1947. Its factory building was completed by the following year, yet production did not begin until 1949, when other factories had already started production. By 1956 there were 113 establishments registered as producing plastic wares, and 15 engaged in the manufacture of bakelite wares, the total employment being about 3,300 workers. As this production does not require any large and heavy machinery, it has become almost a cottage industry, operated on a family basis, so that the number of unregistered establishments probably exceeds 300 and employment well over 5,000.

Most of the raw materials are imported from the United States and Canada. Moulding is the chief method employed. Fully automatic machines are used by large factories. Generally, the capacity of machines ranges from $\frac{1}{2}$ to 5 oz., so that most articles are small in size. Moulding machines producing them are made locally.

The products made by small factories are chiefly consumed locally, and this amounts to about 15 per cent. of the total output. The rest is exported, mainly to Malaya, Africa, and other Commonwealth countries. The value of these exports in 1955 amounted to HK$7.9 million, which constituted 1·1 per cent. of the total value of exports of Hong Kong manufactured goods. In 1956 this item increased to HK$9·7 million. Among the obstacles facing the industry, the growing competition of Japan is the most important. Japanese and Hong Kong plastics compete mainly in Indonesia, Thailand, and Malaya. However, the continuous widening of the range of products and improvements of machinery contribute to the optimistic perspectives for the future of the local plastic industry.

Fountain Pens

The spread of the manufacture and the industrial use of plastics in Hong Kong gave rise, in the last few years, to several new branches of industry. Among them, the production of fountain pens, plastic tooth-brushes, and cameras deserves special attention; other new manufactures are buttons, various bakelite wares, and toys.

The manufacture of fountain pens was first undertaken in Hong Kong by the Kin Wah Pens Factory towards the end of 1949. This factory began with only 18 workers and was not registered until 1953. As business proved satisfactory, this firm quickly expanded, and its success has drawn into this field several entrepreneurs, so that by 1956 there were 5 factories producing fountain pens in the Colony, giving employment to about 200 workers. The output has increased in proportion. The Kin Wah factory alone produced 100–200 dozen pens a day in 1955. A year later it was turning out about 400 dozen pens a day.

The increasing demand, arising from the spread of the fountain-pen habit, was the chief cause of this industry's growth. It started, as many others did, with production for the local market. Soon, however, the export side developed, so that in 1956 only 20 per cent. of the output was sold locally and 80 per cent. abroad, chiefly in China, Singapore, Thailand, and the Philippines. Minor quantities were also exported to Australia, Africa, the British West Indies, Egypt, and Indochina. These markets were captured in spite of very keen competition on the part of the United States, the United Kingdom, Japan, and Western Germany, countries well known for their fountain pens for years.

Cheap labour has undoubtedly played its usual role, especially

as about 65 per cent. of the labour force are women, receiving HK$2·00–3·00 a day. The low cost of raw materials con-
tributed further to the expansion of this industry. The principal
raw material of the holders and caps is plastic cellulose, which
is usually imported from the United Kingdom. The metal from
which the clips of the caps are made is obtained locally. All nibs,
however, have to be imported, mainly from the United States,
as Hong Kong does not yet manufacture them; but it is hoped
that this line of production will be soon undertaken locally.

Tooth-brushes

Until 1949 only hand-made bristle tooth-brushes with bone
handles were manufactured in Hong Kong. China was the
traditional source of the supply of bristle, but with the political
change on the mainland the supplies became erratic and prices
high. This, and the growing popularity of plastics, resulted in an
almost complete switch to the manufacture of tooth-brushes
with plastic handles and nylon tufts; at present only a very small
quantity of bristle tooth-brushes is manufactured in Hong Kong.

In 1956 there were 8 registered firms, ranging from a large,
almost wholly automatic, factory (W. Haking Industries) with
a labour force of 350, to a small establishment operating 3
machines and employing about a dozen workers. Altogether,
460 workers were employed in the registered factories in 1956,
over 50 per cent. of them being women. By 1956 the value of
output increased to about HK$2 million. Substantial quantities
of tooth-brushes were exported to Malaya, the United Kingdom, Canada, New Zealand, Australia, Ceylon, and India.
Parallel with the increase in supply was the fall in price. Heavy
competition on the part of Japan contributed greatly to this decline in price, and imperial preference was an important factor
which enabled the local manufacturers to withstand competition. Some of them, however, found the reduced profit
margin so low that they decided to switch to a new line of production. It was in these circumstances that the largest tooth-
brush factory began the manufacture of cameras.

Photographic Cameras

The pioneer in the manufacture of cameras in Hong Kong
was Mr. Haking Wong, owner of the W. Haking Industries and

former chairman of the Chinese Manufacturers' Union. His venture is an interesting study in entrepreneurship. Mr. Wong has been an amateur photographer since his youth and has read extensively on the subject. During a recent tour overseas he visited various camera factories, and in February 1956 he decided to make cameras in Hong Kong. He began experiments in his own laboratory, then bought machinery mostly from Japan and, after six months' work, his first camera was completed. It was professionally tested and the results proved very successful. This encouraged the producer to design plans for the commercial manufacture of cameras as a new line of the W. Haking Industries (Mechanics and Optics). Towards the end of 1956 production was organized on the scale of 1,000 box cameras and 300 reflex cameras per month.

New equipment is being installed, and output should increase steadily. When full production is reached the monthly output is expected to be 10,000 box cameras and 3,000 reflex cameras. The box camera will retail at HK$16 and the reflex camera at HK$75, while a similar Japanese camera costs HK$115. Thus prices are planned at a level about 35 per cent. below that of the cheapest equivalent cameras known to be produced elsewhere.

The materials for the different parts of the cameras are imported from various countries. The plastic powder for the camera bodies is imported from the United Kingdom and Canada. Brass and other metals for various parts are also ordered from the United Kingdom, while the blanks, or raw material for the lenses, are imported either from Germany or from Japan. All blanks have to be ground, polished, coated, and tested in Hong Kong before mounting. It is hoped that in the course of time the final product will be of 100 per cent. Empire content and will fully qualify for imperial preference.

At the present moment about 60 workers are employed in the manufacture of cameras. Most of them are young women who are working under qualified instructors and mechanics, and are trained to use high-precision machinery. A training programme for 150 more girls is visualized, and it is expected that, after the completion of the training course, they will be paid HK$5 a day.

Sample shipments of the cameras were sent to dealers in the

United Kingdom, the United States, South America, and Australia; and many trial orders have already been received. Other test shipments will be sent to South East Asian markets in the near future. Simultaneously a local sales organization is being built up; and there are good chances that the product will prove to be popular not only with Hong Kong residents but also with tourists visiting the Colony.

Artificial Jewellery

The development of artificial-jewellery manufacture is another instance of innovating entrepreneurial activity. The Colony has a well established production of genuine jewellery and ivory wares. Moreover, there has always been an extensive entrepôt and local trade in various gems, precious stones, and metals. There are about 270 jewellery shops and 12 ivory workshops in Hong Kong, with a considerable number of skilful craftsmen, as even a small jewellery shop employs 4–5 workers. Until recently, the local demand for artificial jewellery was met entirely by imported goods, but the increased demand led to local manufacture being undertaken for the first time in 1951. A more important factor, however, was the response to the needs of local exporters, who had previously handled products manufactured elsewhere.

The industry includes the manufacture of artificial pearls and imitation stones. By 1956 there were 7 factories producing artificial pearls; they engaged 364 workers, mostly women. The workshops are small, usually consisting of a rented flat or a large room occupied by 20–30 workers. Machines are seldom employed and, when used, they are but simple ones, available from Hong Kong machine-manufacturing companies, and are mostly driven by hand. Imitation diamonds are imported from Czechoslovakia and artificial pearls from Japan, but the artificial pearls produced in Hong Kong since 1955 are gradually replacing Japanese pearls. Copper is the main metal used and it is gold or silver plated in the local workshops.

Owing to the competition of foreign artificial jewellery and the prevailing preference of the Colony's ladies for better-quality foreign articles, the products are mostly exported to other countries rather than marketed for local sales. The chief markets are in Indonesia, the Philippines, and South Africa.

Export is usually organized by specialized firms; but some manufacturers sell their jewellery to travelling salesmen who actually take the goods with them to South Africa or South America.

Printing and Publishing

The printing industry in the Colony has a history of more than a hundred years, but for a long time its scale was very limited and its technical methods primitive. The Japanese invasion of China in 1937 caused the first boom in the Hong Kong printing industry. This was partly due to the sudden increase in population and partly to the transfer of printing establishments from China, so that their number in Hong Kong increased in a few years from 240 to more than 300. This flourishing industry was almost swept away during the Japanese occupation. After the war it developed again, and several highly mechanized firms have appeared in recent years.

The total number of workers employed in this industry in 380 registered enterprises in 1956 was almost 7,000, i.e. about 5 per cent. of the total number of workers in registered factories. The industry now consists of commercial printing, newspaper printing (12 establishments in 1955), greeting-cards production, mounting, bookbinding, gilding, engraving, lithography, and the manufacture of printers' ink.

Printing paper, newsprint paper, and printers' ink are the essential raw materials, almost all of which have to be imported, as well as printing machinery. There are some factories producing printers' ink in the Colony, but their output is negligible compared with the volume of imports. The supply of printing materials does not depend on any particular country, but the bulk comes from the United Kingdom, the United States, Canada, Japan, China, and the Netherlands.

Cheap labour and good craftsmanship attract orders from abroad, including even some United Nations agencies, as it is difficult to find better printing establishments in the Far East. But the industry is still far behind international standards, and improvements are necessary.

Paper Manufacture

Before the Second World War, the Tai Shing Paper Mill in Aberdeen, producing 10 tons of paper a day, was the only such mill in the Colony. Because of the shortage of water, the Government bought this mill, including the private water reservoir. The machinery was then sold to a private paper mill in Canton and the reservoir remained the property of the Public Works Department. From that time, no paper mill existed in Hong Kong until a new mill in Un Long (New Territories) was established in 1950, and two other mills in 1951. The demand of the growing local industries, especially printing and publishing, was the main factor which stimulated the reappearance of paper manufacture in Hong Kong. Another favourable element was the high price of paper in international markets—a result of the Korean War.

The basic raw material is waste-paper trimmings obtained from the local printing works, but all the chemicals have to be imported. All three paper mills are equipped with one set of cylinder machinery and, with the exception of waste-paper selecting, paper cutting, and transporting, the whole process is mechanized. As regards output, the Un Long Overseas Paper Mill leads the way. By running 3 shifts it produces $2\frac{1}{2}$ tons a day (1 ton = 16·8 piculs) while the China Paper Mill produces 3–6 piculs and the Hongkong Paper Mill 20–22 piculs a day. About 60 per cent. of the output of the Un Long Mill is exported, chiefly to Singapore, Indonesia, and Macao. The output of the remaining two mills is wholly sold in the local market.

Closely connected with paper manufacture is the production of such articles as paper boxes, lanterns, fans, toys, envelopes, Chinese calendars, and paper drinking-straws. All these products are made almost entirely by hand in small workshops, often at home. As a result, it is difficult to estimate the number of workers in this industry. The official figure for 1956 was 593 in 30 registered establishments. In fact, total employment in the paper industry may well exceed 1,000.

The Film Industry

The film industry in Hong Kong started in 1933, when the Grandview Film Co. was first organized for the production of films in the Cantonese dialect. The industry remained very small for many years, and there were no prospects of further development. The production of films in the Mandarin dialect was not undertaken until after the war in 1947, with the establishment of the Yung Hwa Motion Picture Industries. Between 1947 and 1949 the industry gradually began to grow, but the number of pictures produced was still very small. Then in the boom of 1950–1 Hong Kong produced more than 200 pictures and the industry provided very short-lived jobs for about 50,000 persons. Over 100 motion-picture companies were set up, although they were using the facilities of only 5 or 6 studios in Kowloon. In 1953 Hong Kong ranked as the third largest producer of films in the world after the United States and Japan.

Several factors stimulated this sudden expansion. The deteriorating conditions in Shanghai caused producers of Chinese motion pictures to turn their eyes elsewhere; many of them came to Hong Kong, bringing with them capital, directors, 'stars', technicians, &c. At the same time, when China fell under the Communist rule, her supply of Chinese films to Hong Kong, Singapore, Malaya, Bangkok, and other centres ceased.

Unfortunately, most of the film companies set up during that time closed after their first—and last—film, mainly because they gave too little consideration to quality. It was their practice to invest about HK$50,000 in a production, hoping for quick returns with good profits. The pictures were made within the shortest possible time and at the lowest possible cost. Naturally, only very few ventures proved profitable, and the 1950–1 boom soon ended with the liquidation of most of the companies.

Today there are only 4 companies which have their own studios and 30 other companies which use the facilities, and even the actors, of these 4 big firms. The industry, at present, is employing about 1,000 persons. This includes the directors, actors, producers, technicians, and unskilled labourers. The salaries of directors and producers vary according to their skill and name. Normally they receive a certain percentage of profits per picture, and well-known directors may get over HK$60,000. Permanently employed 'stars' are paid HK$2,500–6,000 per month. 'Stars' engaged on a picture-by-picture basis earn HK$10,000–40,000 per picture, but famous 'stars' demand as much as HK$75,000. Student actors under training get

HK$300–1,000 per month. 'Extras' are hired at HK$5 per day. The technicians' monthly salaries are not very high, ranging from HK$100 to 1,000. Coolies and unskilled workers are paid HK$1 or 2 a day.

The film industry in Hong Kong suffers from lack of talent, up-to-date equipment, and modern technical knowledge. Only the Wader Motion Picture Co. possesses modern equipment imported from Germany, the United Kingdom, and the United States. With one or two exceptions, most of the companies lack working capital. The average cost of producing a Mandarin film is HK$200,000–220,000, while the cost of a Cantonese film comes to about HK$100,000 per picture. Some 40–50 pictures are produced each year, of which about one-quarter are in Mandarin dialect and the remainder in Cantonese. Thus the total output amounts to HK$4–5 million a year.

Most of the films are historical pictures and melodramas, but musical comedies and educational pictures are also produced. Usually the Mandarin films are of a higher standard, but on the whole the quality of pictures is so low that the Hong Kong public shuns local films, and the home market for them is not very large. As a rule, the first-run theatres do not exhibit Chinese pictures, and profits come mainly from overseas markets, Malaya, Singapore, Taiwan, Thailand, Indonesia, Burma, the Philippines, and the United States. Until 1951 Hong Kong films were sent to China, but now only propaganda pictures produced by some companies are admitted. The profits depend on the popularity of the pictures. On the whole, the present profit margin is fairly wide for Cantonese films, which are cheaper to produce and have a larger public. The educated class usually prefers foreign films. As a result, Mandarin films yield relatively low profits or none at all. The industry would gain by amalgamation of the excessive number of firms. By pooling their resources, higher standards and wider markets could be achieved, especially as the Hong Kong film industry is the main source of supply of non-Communist Chinese pictures in Asia.

THE TOURIST INDUSTRY

Hong Kong has not always been 'the brightest jewel in Britain's Far Eastern Crown'. In 1847 a book entitled *China* was published which contained a chapter headed *Hong Kong— Its Position, Prospects, Character and Utter Worthlessness from Every Point of View to England.* Today one can smile at this description, but it must be admitted that in its early days the Colony had an unenviable reputation for rainstorms, typhoons, pirates, poisoners, malaria, dysentery, and other unpleasant scourges. In England at that time contempt for the Colony was expressed in the popular song *You can go to Hong Kong for me.* Today's picture is very different. The Royal Navy has eliminated the pirates; poisoners and other perpetrators of 'crimes against the person' have a healthy respect for a most efficient police force; and the Colony's Medical Department has given Hong Kong up-to-date standards of public health. A visit to modern Hong Kong has become an unforgettable experience to millions of tourists, and money spent by them every year forms a large part of the Colony's income.

In the words of an admirer of the Colony

in the old proverb, all roads led to Rome. In the modern age of air and sea travel very many, if not all, routes lead through Hong Kong. Hundreds of thousands of travellers have lingered in the Colony longer than they have planned; or regretted that they were unable to do so, once they saw for themselves how very beautiful its scenery is, how very interesting the local life, and how comfortable, modern, and convenient the hotels, transportation, and other amenities, at reasonable cost. Exceptionally cheap shopping, with a quickness and quality of service found perhaps nowhere else in the world, is another main point of attraction.[1]

It is estimated that the present volume of business in tourism ranks second only to the textile industry. According to rough calculation, in 1954 a total of HK\$150 million was spent by about 200,000 tourists, who came to Hong Kong from all parts of the world and stayed, on the average, five or six days, whereas a few years ago the average was only about two days. The average figure of individual expenditure was HK\$750 (or about US\$125) a day.[2]

Realizing the attractiveness of the Colony from the visitors' point of view, considerable entrepreneurial effort has been put

[1] E. S. Kirby, 'Hong Kong as a Tourist Centre', *Hongkong Exporter and Far Eastern Importer*, 1955–6.
[2] ibid.

into the provision of tourists' services, hotels, and restaurants. A visitor has the opportunity of enjoying a great variety of Chinese and Western dishes, and he usually does not miss including Aberdeen floating restaurants in his itinerary. In 1954 there were 62 stage and screen theatres, with a total seating capacity of 64,500, of which 10 first-run cinemas accounted for 20,700. By the end of 1955 about 80,000 seats were available. Many of these theatres, as well as other places of entertainment, depend on the very numerous tourists and travellers and on the British and American military personnel. Most visitors do a major part of their shopping during their stay in Hong Kong, buying not merely souvenirs or curios, but also clothing, cameras, watches, or jewellery, because, thanks to the lack of customs duties and to keen competition, prices are exceptionally low.

Various efforts are being made to promote the Colony's tourist industry. Plans are designed for the construction of bigger and better hotels, and the provision of luxury limousines, coaches, and launches. Entry formalities were simplified in August 1955. The newly established Hong Kong Tourist Association should become the distributing centre for the right kind of information on a world-wide basis. Posters, booklets, pamphlets, and films are planned to be sent overseas. The Government, appreciating the economic importance of tourism for the Colony, has recently accepted a plan to spend HK$4 million on promoting it.

The kind of services and goods provided depends largely on the structure of the 'tourist population'. At the moment, its most important element is the American and British army and navy personnel, for whom Hong Kong has been selected as the Far Eastern leave centre. The composition of the tourist flow is, however, changing, and this should result in the provision of new facilities and the adaptation of those already existing.

IV

DYNAMIC BALANCE-SHEET

11

Hong Kong's Political Arithmetic

A HISTORICAL SKETCH

ALTHOUGH the purpose of this study is to describe and analyse the economic growth of Hong Kong during the decade which followed the Second World War, it is impossible to obtain a correct perspective without at least a brief reference to the main trends which preceded the Colony's 'industrial revolution'.

For the first hundred years of its history as a British Crown Colony, Hong Kong was primarily a trading port. Major developments in its early economic history were of a commercial nature. The population gradually increased, as the prosperity of the Colony encouraged immigration from the neighbouring provinces of China and new members of the community brought with them skill in a variety of trades. Consequently there has always been some form of cottage industry in the Colony and, of course, building and construction, land reclamation, transport, &c. Apart from this, Hong Kong's first industries were in the nature of services allied to the development of the port. The earliest was shipbuilding and ship repairing. The first locally built vessel, the *Celestial* of 80 tons, was launched in 1843. It is recorded that a small slip-way capable of taking a vessel of 300 tons was constructed in 1844. By 1860 a large graving dock was in operation at Aberdeen. The project was financed by one of the principal merchant houses. By 1870 increased ship-repairing facilities were constructed on the mainland, and further expansion on the island occurred in 1900.

Towards the end of the nineteenth century three other industrial ventures were launched. Two sugar refineries were established, the first in 1878 and the second in 1882, to satisfy not so much the needs of the then small local population, as the requirements of ships' victualling officers. In 1885 a rope factory was started, again primarily to cater for the seafaring trade. A cement factory was transferred to Hong Kong from Macao in 1899.

From time to time there were tentative efforts to set up other new industries; a spinning mill was started in 1899, but it closed down a few years later. Some industries, however, obtained a firm foothold; in 1902 the manufacture of rattan-ware began, and in 1910 the knitting of cotton singlets and vests became established. These, although flourishing, were almost unnoticeable amid the Colony's growing entrepôt activities. This early industry experienced its ups and downs, partly connected with the recurrent trade depressions, but it was always stimulated by an ample labour supply stemming from the days when Chinese emigration to the Sacramento Valley goldfields, Peru, Jamaica, the West Indies, Malaya, and Australia was channelled through Hong Kong. This abundance of the labour supply was also a most important factor which contributed to the later industrial growth of the Colony.

It was during the period between the First World War and the seizure of the Colony by the Japanese in 1941 that several light industries were established, forerunners of the Colony's economic development after the Second World War. The First World War deprived the Colony of some manufactured goods imported from European sources, and this encouraged the establishment of certain light industries. After the war a weaving factory, operating thirty hand looms, was opened in 1922, and in 1927 the first flashlight manufactory came into being. In 1928 China regained tariff autonomy, and industry in Shanghai and other coastal centres expanded. On the other hand, imports of goods from Hong Kong were handicapped. This factor played a part in retarding the Colony's industrial development.

The Ottawa Agreements of 1932, under which Hong Kong products became entitled to imperial preference, gave the first real encouragement to local industry, enabling manufacturers to seek wider markets for their goods and attracting new investment. The possibility of enlarging local industries was at once foreseen by some far-sighted manufacturers and some imaginative merchants. They planned to combine the dexterity and industry of local workmen with the financial resources and marketing experience of merchant houses. The latter, as a side-line, provided working capital to manufacturers in the form of raw materials such as yarn for the knitting and weaving trades in the garment industry, and rubber, canvas, and chemicals for the rubber-shoe industry. In this way Hong Kong gained a foothold in overseas markets for products for which it has now a world-wide reputation, i.e. yarns, woven textiles, pressure lanterns, rubber footwear, and flashlights, without any form of local tariff protection or strong local demand.

The second stimulus to development was the outbreak of the Second World War in Europe. Some of the orders connected with the war effort were carried out in Hong Kong by the supply of locally built ships, webbing equipment, and other deliveries for military and civilian purposes. It is estimated that in 1940 there were some 800 factories in the Colony, with about 30,000 workers; by the end of 1956 the number of registered and recorded factories increased to 3,319, and employment to 146,877. The rate of growth has thus increased very rapidly in recent years, but it seems that the present widespread industrial development actually started in the 1930s, and was renewed and accelerated after the break caused by the Japanese occupation.

Ever since the Colony's establishment the efficiency of the British administration was a most important factor in Hong Kong's economic development. After the liberation from the Japanese occupation this again became evident. The short period of military administration was followed by what may aptly be defined as Grantham's Era, because the personality of the Governor, Sir Alexander Grantham, became almost a symbol of Hong Kong's stability, and of its economic, social, and cultural progress without any modifications in its political status.

Factory rehabilitation after the war was rapid, urged on by an acute shortage of goods throughout the whole of war-scarred South East Asia. A vital period for local industry was 1948–50, when the influx of refugees from China reached its peak. While most arrived destitute, many brought capital and technical skill which found ready employment in Hong Kong. A minimum of restrictions, a virtual absence of protection, and a high degree of institutional flexibility were the canons of Hong Kong's liberal economic policy. The foreign capitalist or entrepreneur was welcome in the same way as a refugee worker. As a result, post-war Hong Kong, although a British Colony with 98 per cent. of its population Chinese in all walks of life, has a cosmopolitan atmosphere. This policy quickly paid dividends, reflected particularly in the spontaneous growth of manufacturing industry. The development of this industry, the decline in the entrepôt trade with China, and the revolutionary post-war changes in the economy of the Colony have been the main subject of our study.

GENERAL PICTURE OF POST-WAR ECONOMIC GROWTH

The first post-war decade, 1945–55, during which the industrial revolution took place in Hong Kong, can be divided roughly into the following four periods: (1) the reconstruction and rehabilitation period of 1945–7; (2) the initial phase of rapid industrialization, 1947–51; (3) the trade depression of 1951–3; (4) the industrial upswing of 1953–5.

During the first period the Colony was recovering from war destruction, the population was returning from the mainland, industry was rehabilitated, trade connexions were re-established, and all signs indicated that Hong Kong would soon revert to its pre-war position of one of the most important entrepôt centres in the Far East. Then, as conditions were just about to settle 'back to normal', political events in China brought into the Colony a large wave of new labour, capital, and entrepreneurial skill. It was during this second phase that rapid industrialization began. The outbreak of the Korean War retarded this process, because the new speculative trade opportunities attracted a considerable part of the Colony's internal resources, while political uncertainty produced an outflow of some capital abroad. In 1951 the United Nations embargo delivered a heavy blow to entrepôt activities, and the refugees showed no signs of leaving. These were the two main historical reasons which from 1953 onwards speeded up the process of industrialization resumed or begun during the first post-war years. The rate of economic growth was again accelerated; and by 1955 the Colony was showing all the signs of entering the new phase of 'self-sustained growth', to use a Rostowian expression.[1]

Graph V and Tables 42 and 43 (pp. 177–8) provide a general

[1] Rostow, in *Econ. J.*, March 1936, pp. 26–31.

GRAPH V

Main Indicators of Economic Growth

$(1947–8 = 100)$

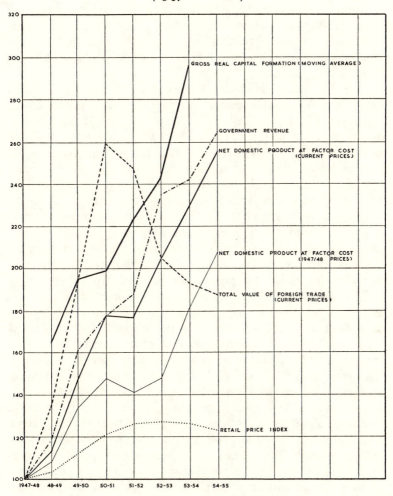

Source: Table 42, Statistical Appendix.

picture of the economic growth of Hong Kong from 1947–8 till 1954–5 in terms of national income and other relevant magnitudes.[1] Among the four phases of Hong Kong's post-war economic growth, the first (post-war recovery) is interesting in so far as it prepared the ground for the subsequent industrial take-off. Unfortunately, lack of statistical data prevents any attempt at quantitative estimates of the rates of growth during this early period. For this reason, a more detailed analysis must begin with the initial phase of industrialization, from 1947–8 to 1950–1.

The position of the economy in 1947–8 may be characterized by a Net National Product (at Factor Cost) approximately equal to HK\$1,600 million. By 1950–1 the Net National Product of the Colony increased to about HK\$2,800 million (HK\$2,300 in 1947–8 prices). During four years, therefore, the nominal National Product increased by about 75 per cent., giving an average rate of growth equal to 19 per cent. p.a. The rate of growth in real terms amounted to 44 per cent. over 4 years, i.e. 10–11 per cent. p.a. on the average. In the words of Harrod, 'without any great revolution, *G* (rate of national-income growth) might easily change from 2 to 6 per cent'[2]. But an average increase of income exceeding 10 per cent. p.a. *in real terms* should be regarded as a revolutionary change.

The Korean boom of 1950–1 had manifold effects on the economy of Hong Kong. A speculative rise in prices almost produced a balance of the value of imports and exports in 1950, and in 1950–1 the total volume of trade reached its post-war peak. The Colony was at a peak of prosperity. However, attractive gains in foreign trade retarded the rate of industrialization. Even building activity was at a comparatively low level. Then came the slump resulting from the imposition of the embargo. As a result, between 1950–1 and 1951–2 the national income in real terms declined by about 4 per cent. Depression began to spread, the excess of imports over exports increased from 9 to 24 per cent. of the national income, and capital was leaving the Colony in pursuit of more profitable and safer investment abroad.

---

[1] Most of these data are only rough estimates. Cf. notes accompanying these tables.

[2] R. F. Harrod, *Towards a Dynamic Economics* (London, Macmillan, 1948), p. 79.

It was in this situation that another source for financing the industrial growth of Hong Kong became available as the entrepôt traders switched to industrial investment. Stocks of goods were liquidated, sometimes at considerable loss, and profits accumulated during the Korean boom were directed to new industrial enterprises. Building and construction also absorbed a large part of these funds, and the index of real-capital formation rose from 168 in 1951–2 to 311 in 1952–3. The rate of money-income growth went up to about 14 per cent. because of the multiplier-effects of the investments. In order to provide the necessary capital goods in this new phase of industrialization, retained imports had to increase considerably, and in 1952–3 the excess of imports over exports rose to about 31 per cent. of the national income, from 24 per cent. in the preceding year.

Between 1953 and 1955 the economy adjusted itself to the low level of entrepôt trade, and the switch to manufacturing industries as the main source of the national income became an accomplished fact. A major factor during the early part of this period was the war in Indochina, which, combined with the political tension in the Straits of Formosa, produced a situation of uncertainty in the Far East. In spite of this, industrialization was progressing, favoured by some influx of capital from Indochina and other neighbouring countries, and the rate of growth of the national income amounted to 12 per cent. per annum. The industrial foundations of the Colony were thus further strengthened and widened, and a year later returns began to come in, in the form of a substantial increase in the export of local products. Simultaneously, gradual political stabilization in the Far East gave rise to an increased flow of capital into Hong Kong as the industrial expansion began to attract investors from abroad, mainly from Singapore, Indochina, and the Philippines.

The best indications of prosperity were the increase in real-capital formation from HK$234 million in 1953–4 to HK$318 million in 1954–5, and the increase of the Government's revenue from HK$397 to HK$434 million during the same period. According to the estimates presented in Table 44, the national product of the Colony in 1954–5 amounted to approximately HK$4,000 million, about one-third of it being derived from manufacturing industry. The national output per head reached the figure of approximately HK$1,700 per annum, the equivalent of US$300 or £106, one of the highest in the Far East.[1]

To a considerable extent, this high level of Hong Kong's economic prosperity has been due to the process of industrialization on which attention was concentrated in this book. But the picture would be distorted if we did not stress the importance of the recent recovery in entrepôt trade, particularly in 1955-6. A most significant feature of this recovery was the change in the composition and direction of Hong Kong's entrepôt trade. Table 45 (pp. 179–82) illustrates these changes. The principal items of entrepôt trade are now textiles, clothing, textile fibres, metal manufactures, i.e. a wide range of manufactured consumer goods in popular demand, particularly all over the Far East and South East Asia, whereas traditional trade in Chinese products, such as tea, silk, vegetable oils, nuts, spices, oilseeds, and other vegetable and animal products has considerably declined at least in relative, if not in absolute, terms. The change in the direction of trade is best illustrated by the decline of the Colony's exports to China to about 4 per cent. of Hong Kong's total exports in 1956, whereas only a quarter of a century ago (i.e. before the introduction of imperial preference) almost 60 per cent. of Hong Kong's exports were sent to China. Other countries, such as Indonesia, Malaya, Thailand, Japan, the United Kingdom, Indochina, South Korea, the United States, and various African countries, have taken the place of China. The accompanying increase in the volume of the entrepôt trade in recent years is becoming an important factor in financing the Colony's industrial development.

FINANCING THE PROCESS OF GROWTH

Throughout this book we have examined the mechanism and the various factors explaining the industrial revolution in Hong Kong. There is still, however, one intriguing question which so

[1] In 1952–4 the annual average *per capita* net national product amounted to US$310 in Malaya, US$190 in Japan, US$150 in the Philippines, US$110 in Ceylon, US$80 in Thailand, US$70 in Korea and in Pakistan, US$60 in India, and US$50 in Burma (United Nations, Statistical Office, *Per Capita National Product of Fifty-five Countries: 1952–1954*, (New York, 1957), Statistical Papers, Series E, no. 4, p. 7).

far has not been raised, viz. what was the magnitude and origin of the investment involved? It is impossible to give an exact answer, but the calculations presented in Table 46 (p. 183) provide at least a method of approach and rough limits within which a more precise solution could be found.

The analysis is based on a modified version of the Harrodian 'growth equation', which relates the rate of income growth to the rate of saving and the capital/output ratio, that is to say the ratio between the increment in capital (investment) and the resulting addition to output at the margin. The modification consists in the introduction of the inflow of capital from abroad as the second source of finance in addition to local savings. Furthermore, for statistical convenience, it was necessary to separate the balance of trade in merchandise from the balance of 'invisible' items (including governmental and private transfers [1]) which in Hong Kong have always been of great importance. [2]

In view of the inadequacy of statistical data, a number of assumptions had to be introduced so that the results presented in Table 46 have the character of tentative estimates rather than of statistical series. Thus the estimated rate of income growth during 1947–55, and the balance of trade as a fraction of national income, were taken from Table 42 (p. 177), to which reference has already been made. The rate of saving has been assumed as equal to about 10 per cent. of the national income. [3] The estimation of the capital/output ratio presented great difficulties. According to available studies, it is usually a fairly stable, technically determined coefficient, normally fluctuating between 2 and 4, but there are large discrepancies in its value between various countries and industries. No studies of capital/output ratio in Hong Kong have been undertaken, but the present writer has experimented with several hypothetical

---

[1] Governmental transfers on the whole produced a negative balance during the period under consideration, as most of the surpluses and various reserve funds were being invested abroad. Private transfers on current account, consisting chiefly of aid to families in China, were also negative.

[2] No allowance was made for the trade in gold. Controlled gold and specie movements in Hong Kong do not show any significant import or export surpluses. It is impossible to estimate the smuggling.

[3] Cf. Szczepanik, *Cost of Living*, p. 5, and *National Income*, p. 56. Closer estimates of the rate of saving are unobtainable because of the importance of unincorporated enterprises in the Colony's national income.

values of this coefficient and has come to the conclusion that the assumption of it being equal to 2 is the most plausible one. Such a low capital/output ratio seems to reflect the fact that quick returns were the mainspring and *sine qua non* of investment in the Colony.[1]

Table 46 (p. 183) shows the tentative values of invisible earnings and of the inflow of capital from abroad during the period 1947–55. The most interesting conclusion resulting from the analysis of this table is that the average sum of invisible earnings and of the inflow of capital from abroad throughout this period amounted to about 40 per cent. of the national income. There were only two major deviations from this figure. One occurred between 1948–9 and 1949–50, when this ratio was as high as 65 per cent., reflecting the magnitude of refugee capital which arrived in the Colony at that time. The second opposite deviation from the average occurred between 1950–1 and 1951–2, when this ratio fell to 6·5 per cent. as a result of the post-Korean depression aggravated by the embargo, which produced an outflow of capital and a decline in invisible earnings.

In absolute terms, the average annual inflow of capital from abroad together with invisible earnings during the period under examination amounted to about HK$1,000 million, the equivalent of £65 million. The distinction between invisible earnings and inflow of capital from abroad (if we neglect the balance of governmental transfers) is very difficult, but according to a fairly uniform opinion prevailing in the Colony, the annual inflow of capital was in the region of HK$300–600 million in recent years and was even larger during the period of 1948–50. Thus the invisible earnings of the Colony probably amounted to about HK$500 million in 1948–50 and about HK$1,000 million in the middle 1950's.

Table 46 also shows that these two sources, invisible earnings and inflow of capital from abroad, were large enough to finance the substantial import surplus of the Colony. Only during the depression period of 1951–2 did a net deficit in the overall balance of payments occur amounting to about HK$300

---

[1] The author is fully aware of the need for statistical verification of the value of this coefficient, and for sectorial analysis which is the subject of his planned future research.

million. Otherwise, the average surplus of approximately HK$400 million (about £25 million) was built up each year on the external-payments account, thus permitting the financing of industrial investment in both fixed and working capital to such an extent that the rate of growth of the economy had revolutionary dimensions indeed.

Finally, it appears from this analysis that the part played by internal savings was comparatively small. Approximately one-third of investment was financed by internal savings, the remaining two-thirds by capital from abroad. This stands up to logic and to facts. At the start of the industrialization process, Hong Kong had a war-devastated economy, with a very unequal income distribution. Not much more than HK$150 million could have been saved in 1947–8. As during 1947–8 about HK$95 million was invested in buildings and machinery, only about HK$55 million was left from savings for working capital, not enough to employ a labour force of more than 45,000, i.e. only a very small part of the total industrial labour force at that time. The excess of imports over exports amounted to HK$424 million. Thus the inflow of capital from abroad must be added, for invisible earnings were probably just enough to balance the payments. The rest of the incoming capital went to finance investment in connexion with the industrialization process. This pattern, with some variations, was roughly followed throughout the whole period under review.

PROSPECTS FOR FUTURE GROWTH

In spite of various inevitable deficiencies and inaccuracies the above analysis makes possible some conclusions as to the prospects of the Colony's future growth. The period of eight years of industrial revolution, 1947–55, was characterized by a relatively high rate of income growth, which in the last few years continued to be approximately 12 per cent. per annum. This rate of growth was possible thanks to a comparatively large inflow of capital from abroad, substantial invisible earnings, the absence of inflationary tendencies, and the continued switch from entrepôt trading to manufacturing industry.

In view of a rate of population growth already exceeding 3 per cent. p.a., the minimum conditions of economic progress in the Colony would be a rate of income growth equal to 4 per cent. p.a. Assuming that the capital/output ratio continues to be 2, the rate of saving 10 per cent., and the import surplus as a fraction of national income equal to 27 per cent., then, in the absence of further inflow of capital from abroad, and assuming a balance on the governmental transfers account, the invisible earnings should amount to about one-quarter of the national income, in order to pay for the imports necessary to sustain the 4 per cent. rate of growth.[1] This is a very high ratio.

This ratio could be lower, without affecting the Colony's material progress, under any of the following conditions:

1. The balance of trade as a fraction of national income may improve. But in view of the shortage of raw materials in the Colony it is most unlikely that it will fall below 10 per cent. of national income, which was approximately the minimum value of this ratio during the 1950–1 boom. On this optimistic assumption the minimum equilibrium value of invisible earnings as a fraction of income would be 8 per cent.

2. The rate of saving may increase. But even as high an increase as from 10 to 15 per cent. would reduce, *ceteris paribus*, the normative equilibrium value of invisible earnings as a fraction of income to only 20 per cent.

3. The present rate of population growth may decline, which would reduce the necessary rate of income growth below the assumed 4 per cent. p.a. Although this seems to be a very unrealistic assumption, it must be stressed that any decline in the current high rate of population growth would be beneficial to the increase of material welfare of the Colony. The current rate, 3 per cent. p.a., is very high, and some limitation of this expansionary tendency might be considered.

On the other hand, invisible earnings as a fraction of income may have to become larger than the above calculated 25 per cent. minimum owing to the following reasons:

---

[1] If, as in Table 46, we denote

rate of income growth $= G = 4\%$
capital/output ratio $= C = 2$
rate of saving $= s = 10\%$
import surplus as a fraction of income $= b = 27\%$
and the sum of capital inflow from abroad and invisible earnings (expressed as a fraction of income) $= f$
then $f = GC - s + b = 4\% \times 2 - 10\% + 27\% = 25\%$

1. The necessary minimum rate of income growth may have to be far above the assumed 4 per cent. p.a. should there be a continuation of the influx of population from China. This is a most important consideration. As has been mentioned before, the 1948–50 influx of refugees brought into Hong Kong not only labour but also capital and entrepreneurial skill. However, any new influx of population from Communist China would not be accompanied by capital. Thus, putting aside humanitarian aspects, the Colony's policy should be not to allow any further immigration from the mainland. This is, in fact, what is being done now. Pursuance of this immigration policy is an obvious prerequisite for the future economic progress of Hong Kong.

2. The capital/output ratio may well increase to 3 or 4 with a change in the nature of investment. There are signs that the Colony's infrastructure, flexible as it was during the first post-war decade, has been stretched to such an extent that considerable investment for the purpose of developing it may soon become an inevitable necessity. But if the capital/output ratio increases to, say, 4, then invisible earnings would have to amount, *ceteris paribus*, to 65 per cent. of the national income.[1]

So far we have been concentrating only on invisible earnings, assuming the absence of inflow of capital from abroad and the usual *ceteris paribus* clause. There is, of course, no reason to retain these assumptions:

1. A substantial reduction in the necessary rate of invisible earnings would be possible if Hong Kong were to receive further injections of capital from abroad. Although some inflow of capital into the Colony in the years to come cannot be excluded, it is difficult to make any prediction. Throughout the whole first post-war decade the Colony has been a refuge for Far Eastern investors, and there are grounds to believe that it will continue to perform this role. So far, however, there has been no specific effort to ensure this flow. It seems that more attractive rates on bank deposits, development of investment trusts, finance corporations, building societies, &c., could be important elements in attracting more capital from abroad.

2. This leads further to the conclusion that, if necessary, the

---

[1] Instead of discussing this possibility in terms of rising capital/output ratio, reference could be made to the necessity of taking into account capital widening and/or deepening.

Government may play an important role in the mobilization of capital; the transfer of the Government's overseas investment into the Colony would be of great importance, the possibility of floating government loans abroad should not be excluded, and an internal loan would help considerably to mobilize idle money and re-direct speculative funds.

3. Of minor importance, although growing with time, may be the decline in the volume of transfers to China. A large part of these transfers consists of family aid, and it would be reasonable to assume that, as time goes on, family ties between people in Hong Kong and on the mainland will gradually become less binding and the internal social cohesion will increase.

Finally, the Colony's invisible earnings themselves might well grow through an increase in the income from the numerous entrepôt activities, shipping, aviation, insurance, banking, &c. The development of Kai Tak Airport and the expansion of local aircraft companies may be important elements in this respect. The expansion of tourism also seems to be one of the most promising lines for increasing the Colony's invisible earnings.

To conclude, there are various reasons for optimism regarding the economy of Hong Kong assuming the continuity of its present political stability. But much depends on how future economic policy will tackle the main problems presented above. So far, this policy has been formed spontaneously, as a result of individual entrepreneurial decisions. The present author hopes that this book may contribute towards more co-ordinated thinking in macroeconomic terms.

STATISTICAL APPENDIX

TABLE I

The Pattern of Government Expenditure, 1952–3 to 1955–6

	Percentage of the total
ECONOMIC SERVICES:	
Public Works Department	17·6
Post Office	3·2
Marine Department	2·4
Civil Aviation	1·6
Store Department	1·6
Commerce & Industry Department . . .	1·0
Agriculture, Fisheries, & Forestry Department . .	0·7
Royal Observatory	0·3
Co-operatives & Marketing Department . . .	0·4
Labour Department	0·2
Miscellaneous (including K.C.R.) . . .	2·0
	—— 31·0
SOCIAL SERVICES:	
Education	10·1
Medical & health services	9·3
Urban (sanitary) services	3·8
Social welfare	2·9
Resettlement Department	1·1
Fire Brigade	0·7
Broadcasting Department	0·2
Secretariat for Chinese Affairs	0·1
Subventions	0·1
	—— 28·3
ADMINISTRATION	18·7
MAINTENANCE OF LAW AND ORDER:	
Police	10·1
Prisons	1·5
Judiciary	0·6
Legal Department	0·2
Registrar General's Department	0·2
District Watch Force	0·1
	—— 12··
DEFENCE:	
Contribution to the maintenance of the British Forces & other defence measures	6·9
Hong Kong Defence Force	1·2
Registration of persons (under Defence Regulations) .	0·1
	—— 8·2
PUBLIC DEBT SERVICE	1·1
TOTAL	100·0

Sources: Accountant General, *Annual Departmental Reports,* and *Estimates of Revenue and Expenditure.*

TABLE 2

The Pattern of Government Revenue, 1952–3 to 1955–6 (Percentages of total)

Source of revenue	1952–3	1953–4	1954–5	1955–6	Average 1952–3 to 1956
TAX REVENUE					
Internal revenue:					
Earnings & profits tax	29·0	28·8	24·7	21·4	25·9
Stamp duties	3·7	3·7	4·2	4·8	4·2
Entertainment tax	2·4	2·4	2·1	2·2	2·3
Bets & sweeps tax	2·7	2·6	2·0	1·8	2·2
Estate duty	1·6	1·0	2·8	1·5	1·7
Business registration tax	1·5	0·9	1·7	1·2	1·3
Meals & liquors tax	0·8	0·8	0·7	0·5	0·7
Dance-halls tax	0·2	0·2	0·3	0·4	0·3
	41·9	40·4	38·5	33·8	38·6
Duties:					
Import duties	16·1	15·7	15·2	15·6	15·7
Duties	3·2	3·1	3·0	3·1	3·1
Rates	19·3	18·8	18·2	18·7	18·8
Fees of court or office	8·9	9·5	9·2	10·9	9·6
Licences, fines, & forfeitures	6·9	7·1	8·6	7·3	7·5
Misc. receipts (mostly royalties)	4·7	4·4	3·4	4·1	4·1
	3·9	3·7	4·8	4·6	4·3
	85·6	83·9	82·7	79·4	82·9
GOVERNMENT TRADING ACTIVITIES					
Lease & rent of Crown land	4·9	5·8	5·8	6·9	5·8
Post Office	4·0	5·0	5·2	5·4	4·9
Sale of land	1·4	1·5	2·8	3·0	2·2
Water revenue	2·2	2·2	1·8	2·1	2·1
Kowloon–Canton Railway	1·6	1·4	1·1	1·2	1·3
	14·1	15·9	16·7	18·6	16·3
OTHER SOURCES OF CURRENT REVENUE					
Colonial Development & Welfare Fund	0·3	0·2	0·3	0·2	0·2
Loans from U.K. Government			0·3	1·8	0·6
	0·3	0·2	0·6	2·0	0·8
TOTAL	100·0	100·0	100·0	100·0	100·0

Sources: Accountant General, *Annual Departmental Reports*, and *Estimates of Revenue and Expenditure.*

TABLE 3

Government Expenditure, 1952–3 to 1955–6
(Percentages of total)

Expenditure	1952–3	1953–4	1954–5	1955–6
Economic services .	30·7	27·1	31·1	34·7
Social services	23·5	25·9	29·2	34·5
Administration	19·6	24·7	18·4	12·3
Law & order	13·6	12·7	12·4	11·9
Defence	10·8	8·5	8·0	5·8
Public debt service	1·8	1·1	0·9	0·8
TOTAL .	100·0	100·0	100·0	100·0

Sources: Accountant General, *Annual Departmental Reports,* and *Estimates of Revenue and Expenditure.*

TABLE 4

Government Revenue and Expenditure, 1947–8 to 1955–6
(HK$ million)

Year	Revenue	Expenditure	Surplus
1947–8	164	128	36
1948–9	195	160	35
1949–50	264	182	82
1950–1	292	252	40
1951–2	309	276	33
1952–3	385	312	73
1953–4	397	355	42
1954–5	434	373	61
1955–6	455	402	53

Source: Hong Kong Annual Reports.

TABLE 5

The Supply of Cash, 1950–6
(HK$ million—rounded figures)

Year	Hongkong & Shanghai Banking Corporation	Chartered Bank	Mercantile Bank of India	Government		Total
				One dollar notes	Subsidiary notes & coins	
1950	753	45	3·9	40·9	10·9	854
1951	756	46	4·3	28·1	14·9	849
1952	756	38	4·1	23·5	17·6	840
1953	756	40	4·4	24·7	17·5	843
1954	756	44	4·3	25·0	17·4	846
1955	676	47	4·1	27·7	17·2	772
1956	676	52	3·5	33·4	18·2	783

Sources: The above statistics refer to 31 March of each year and are based on *Hong Kong Government Gazette*, Supplement no. 4, and Accountant General, *Annual Departmental Reports*.

TABLE 6

Estimated Growth of Population, 1931–41

1931	.	.	.	.	840,473	1937 .	.	.	.	1,281,982
1932	.	.	.	.	900,812	1938 .	.	.	.	1,478,619
1933	.	.	.	.	922,643	1939 .	.	.	.	1,750,256
1934	.	.	.	.	944,492	1940 .	.	.	.	1,821,893
1935	.	.	.	.	966,341	1941 .	.	.	.	1,639,357
1936	.	.	.	.	988,190					

Source: Director of Medical and Health Services, *Annual Departmental Report, 1950–1*, p. 9.

TABLE 7

Estimated Growth of Population, 1945–56

Mid-year	Total population	Number of births	Number of deaths	Birth rate	Death rate
1945	500,000–600,000	3,712	23,098	?	?
1946	1,168,000	31,098	16,653	26·6	14·2
1947	1,214,000	42,473	13,231	35·0	10·9
1948	1,310,000	47,475	13,434	36·3	10·1
1949	1,415,000	54,774	16,287	38·7	11·5
1950	1,670,000	60,600	18,465	36·2	11·1
1951	1,846,000	68,500	20,580	37·1	11·1
1952	1,967,000	71,976	19,459	36·6	9·9
1953	2,050,000	75,544	18,300	36·9	9·0
1954	2,120,000	83,317	19,823	39·3	9·3
1955	2,250,000	90,511	19,080	40·0	8·4
1956	2,400,000	96,746	19,295	40·0	8·0

Source: Szczepanik, 'The Hong Kong Population Puzzle', *Far East. Econ. R.*, 29 September 1955. Data for 1955–6 have been supplemented later by the author. The population at the end of 1956 was estimated by the Government to be about 2,535,000, excluding service personnel and their families (*Hong Kong Annual Report 1956*, p. 31).

TABLE 8

Estimates of Net Immigration, 1945–56

Year	Mid-year population	Total increase	Natural increase (calendar years)	Adjusted natural increase (mid-year period)	Net immigration (mid-year periods)
1945	500,000–600,000		−19,377		
		600,000(?)		?	600,000(?)
1946	1,168,000		14,445		
		46,000		21,000	25,000
1947	1,214,000		29,242		
		96,000		31,000	65,000
1948	1,310,000		34,041		
		105,000		36,000	70,000
1949	1,415,000		38,487		
		255,000		40,000	215,000
1950	1,670,000		42,135		
		176,000		45,000	130,000
1951	1,846,000		47,920		
		121,000		50,000	70,000
1952	1,967,000		52,517		
		83,000		55,000	28,000
1953	2,050,000		57,244		
		70,000		60,000	10,000
1954	2,120,000		63,494		
		130,000		67,000	63,000
1955	2,250,000		71,431		
		150,000		74,000	76,000
1956	2,400,000		77,451		

Source: Szczepanik, in *Far East. Econ. R.*, 29 September 1955. Data for 1955–6 have been supplemented later by the author.

TABLE 9

Occupational Structure of Immigrants
(Working-age population only)

Occupation	Percentage of the total immigrant population	
	According to occupation in China	According to occupation in Hong Kong
Farmers	9·6	1·6
Fishermen	0·2	0·2
Coolies & domestic servants . . .	0·8	11·0
Cottage craftsmen	1·4	9·5
Industrial labourers	2·7	12·6
Independent craftsmen	1·9	2·7
Hawkers	2·4	7·4
Clerks & shop assistants	9·9	5·3
Business men	5·3	1·6
Professionals & intellectuals . . .	10·0	3·5
Army & police	16·4	0·2
Others	4·7	4·8
Unemployed	2·0	15·1
Housewives	32·7	24·5
TOTAL	100·0	100·0

Source: Hambro Report, Tables xxix and xxxi.

TABLE 10

Sales and Prices of Fish, 1946–7 to 1954–5

(Index numbers, 1947–8 = 100)

Year	Quantity of fish marketed through FMO	Wholesale prices of fresh fish
1946–7	98	133
1947–8	100	100
1948–9	155	104
1949–50	188	144
1950–1	194	120
1951–2	197	119
1952–3	227	94
1953–4	216	117
1954–5	268	84

Source: Registrar of Co-operative Societies and Director of Marketing, *Annual Departmental Report, 1954–5.*

TABLE 11

Foreign Trade, 1946–56

(1948 = 100)

Year	Import		Export		Total		Balance of Trade	
	HK$ m.	Index	HK$ m.	Index	HK$ m.	Index	HK$ m.	Index
1946	933	45	766	48	1,699	46	− 168	34
1947	1,550	75	1,217	77	2,767	76	− 333	67
1948	2,078	100	1,583	100	3,660	100	− 495	100
1949	2,750	132	2,319	146	5,069	138	− 431	87
1950	3,788	182	3,716	235	7,503	205	− 72	14
1951	4,870	234	4,433	280	9,303	254	− 437	88
1952	3,779	182	2,899	183	6,678	182	− 880	178
1953	3,873	186	2,734	173	6,606	180	−1,139	230
1954	3,435	165	2,417	153	5,852	160	−1,018	206
1955	3,719	179	2,534	160	6,253	171	−1,185	239
1956	4,566	220	3,210	203	7,776	213	−1,356	274

Sources: Hong Kong Trade Returns, 1946–53; Hong Kong Trade Statistics, 1954–6.

TABLE 12

Cargo Discharged and Loaded, 1947–56

Year	Total tonnage	Index of the total (1948 = 100)
1947	3,522,644	86
1948	4,098,028	100
1949	5,494,963	134
1950	7,106,139	173
1951	5,871,183	143
1952	5,085,870	124
1953	5,011,820	122
1954	5,185,495	126
1955	5,896,367	144
1956	6,653,088	162

Source: Director of Marine Department and General Manager of the Kowloon–Canton Railway, *Annual Departmental Reports.* (Volume data for 1946 are not available.)

TABLE 13

Value of Post-war Trade Adjusted for Price Changes, 1948–55

Year	Wholesale price index	Total value of trade at current prices (HK$ million)	Adjusted value of total trade at 1948 prices (HK$ million)	Adjusted total trade value index
1948	100	3,660	3,660	100
1949	91	5,069	5,595	153
1950	103	7,503	7,313	200
1951	158	9,303	5,873	160
1952	124	6,678	5,381	147
1953	89	6,606	7,423	203
1954	81	5,852	7,261	198
1955	90	6,253	6,947	190

Sources: Hong Kong Trade Returns, 1948–53; *Hong Kong Trade Statistics,* 1954–5. The index is based on the following items, weighted to correspond with 1948 values of total trade (exports plus imports): cotton yarn 38·3; tung oil 24·9; sugar 14·7; grey sheeting 9·9; newsprint 8·9; caustic soda 3·3.

Prices were taken as annual averages calculated from the data published in Hong Kong in the *Daily Commodity Quotations,* the *Wah Kiu Yat Po Year-book,* and *Far East. Econ. R.*

TABLE 14

Trade with China, 1931–40 and 1946–56
(HK$ million)

Year	Exports to China	Total exports from Hong Kong	Imports from China	Total imports of Hong Kong	Exports to China as a percentage of total value of HK's exports	Imports from China as a percentage of total value of HK's imports
1931	299	547	199	737	52·8	27·0
1932	280	472	170	624	59·3	27·2
1933	227	403	155	501	56·3	30·9
1934	156	325	146	416	48·0	35·1
1935	133	271	123	365	49·1	33·7
1936	150	351	152	452	42·2	33·6
1937	190	467	211	617	40·7	34·2
1938	231	512	233	618	45·1	37·7
1939	90	533	224	595	16·9	37·6
1940	155	622	257	753	24·9	34·1
1946	301	766	327	933	39·3	35·1
1947	265	1,217	376	1,550	21·8	24·3
1948	280	1,583	431	2,077	17·7	20·7
1949	585	2,319	593	2,750	25·2	21·5
1950	1,460	3,716	860	3,788	39·3	22·7
1951	1,604	4,433	863	4,870	36·2	17·6
1952	520	2,899	830	3,779	18·3	21·9
1953	540	2,734	857	3,873	19·7	22·1
1954	391	2,417	692	3,435	16·2	20·2
1955	182	2,534	897	3,719	7·2	24·1
1956	136	3,210	1,038	4,566	4·2	22·7

Sources: Hong Kong Trade and Shipping Returns, 1931–40; Hong Kong Trade Returns, 1946–53; Hong Kong Trade Statistics, 1954–6. (Figures for Taiwan are excluded for the years 1951–6.)

TABLE 15

Number of Registered and Recorded Factories and Industrial Workers, 1940–56

(1948 = 100)

Year	Factories		Workers	
	Number	*Index*	*Number*	*Index*
1940	800	63	30,000	47
1947	972	77	51,338	80
1948	1,266	100	63,873	100
1949	1,426	113	81,571	128
1950	1,752	138	91,986	144
1951	1,961	155	95,207	149
1952	2,088	165	98,126	153
1953	2,208	174	100,776	158
1954	2,494	197	115,453	180
1955	2,925	231	129,465	203
1956 (June)	3,204	253	144,581	226

Source: Commissioner of Labour, *Annual Departmental Reports.*

TABLE 16

Employment in Registered and Recorded Factories, 1955
(Percentages of total)

Industry	Percentage
Textiles	28·43
Metal products except machinery, transport, & equipment	13·28
Transport equipment	9·09
Electrical machinery, apparatus, appliances, & supplies .	7·07
Rubber products	6·39
Printing, publishing, & allied industries . . .	5·33
Food manufacturing industries, except beverages . .	5·20
Footwear, other wearing apparel, & made-up textile goods	5·20
Chemicals & chemical products	2·65
Machinery, except electrical machinery	1·93
Non-metallic products, except products of petroleum and coal	1·83
Wood & cork, except furniture	1·49
Basic metal industries	1·42
Electricity, gas, & steam	1·11
Tobacco manufactures.	1·06
Personal services (laundries)	1·04
Beverage industries	0·79
Communications	0·70
Metal mining	0·52
Furniture & fixtures	0·51
Commerce (petroleum installations)	0·41
Paper & paper products	0·36
Storage & warehousing	0·35
Recreation services (motion pictures production) . .	0·31
Leather & leather products, except footwear . . .	0·20
Stone quarrying, clay & sand quarrying not elsewhere classified	0·10
Construction (terrazzo works)	0·07
Transport (packing cargo)	0·05
Manufacture of products of petroleum & coal . .	0·01
Miscellaneous manufacturing industries	3·23
TOTAL	100·00

Source: Commissioner of Labour, *Annual Departmental Report, 1954–5.*

TABLE 17

Employment Structure, June 1954

Employment	Percentage of the working-age population	Percentage of the total population	Numbers (rounded figures)
Farmers	4·0	2·3	51,000
Fishermen	1·0	0·6	13,000
Coolies & amahs	9·6	5·5	120,000
Cottage craftsmen	7·1	4·0	88,000
Industrial labourers . . .	11·2	6·4	140,000
Independent craftsmen . . .	3·4	2·0	44,000
Hawkers	7·4	4·2	92,000
Clerks & shop assistants . . .	5·9	3·4	75,000
Business men	1·9	1·1	24,000
Professionals & intellectuals . .	2·6	1·5	33,000
Army and police	1·0	0·6	13,000
Others	5·2	3·0	66,000
Total gainfully employed population	60·6	35·0	760,000
Unemployed	12·2	7·0	150,000
Housewives	27·2	16·0	350,000
Total working-age population .	100·0	57·4	1,265,000
Children:			
0–4 (below school age) . .		14·8	325,000
5–14 (school age):			
in recognized schools . .			230,000
in unrecognized schools . .			75,000
not receiving any education .			230,000
Total children of school age . .		24·4	535,000
Old-age persons (above 60) . .		3·4	75,000
GRAND TOTAL . . .		100·0	2,200,000

Source: Hambro Report. (For the sake of rounding, total population was taken as 2,200,000 in June 1954.)

TABLE 18

Structure of Exports of Hong Kong Products, 1955–6
(*Percentages of total value*)

Product			1955	1956
Textiles	*1955*	*1956*		
Cotton piece-goods . . .	24·9	22·1		
Cotton yarns	13·7	12·5		
Cotton singlets . . .	8·1	9·6		
Shirts	9·0	9·1		
Towels, not embroidered .	1·8	1·8		
Linen, embroidered . .	1·2	1·4		
Outerwear, embroidered . .	0·9	0·9		
Clothing (other), embroidered .	0·5	0·8		
Underwear and nightwear, embroidered	0·4	0·4		
			60·5	58·6
Footwear			14·3	9·8
Household utensils, enamelled .			7·7	9·7
Electric torches			6·9	6·4
Foodstuffs & beverages . .			2·2	2·5
Lanterns, metal . . .			1·8	2·2
Lacquer varnishes, paint, enamel, &c.			1·7	1·9
Iron and steel bars . . .			1·2	1·9
Plastic articles			1·1	1·2
Household utensils, aluminium .			1·3	1·1
Torch batteries			1·2	1·1
Vacuum flasks			1·1	1·0
Cement			0·9	1·0
Torch bulbs			0·8	0·8
Iron & tungsten ore . . .			0·6	0·6
Matches			0·3	0·1
Cigarettes			0·1	0·1
Seagrass			—	—
Beer			—	—
TOTAL			100·0	100·0

Source: Hong Kong Trade Statistics, 1955–6.

TABLE 19

Family Expenditure in Hong Kong and in the United Kingdom

Item	U.K. Survey 1953–4, at January 1956 prices	Hong Kong Survey, December 1955, at current prices
Food & drink	42·1	53·83
Housing	8·7	9·64
Clothing & footwear . . .	10·6	5·35
Fuel & light	5·5	7·23
Tobacco & cigarettes . . .	8·0	4·89
Transport & vehicles . . .	6·8	2·52
Household equipment . . .	6·6	0·95
Other items	11·7	15·59
TOTAL	100·00	100·00

Sources: The Economist, 17 March 1956, and Szczepanik, *Cost of Living*, p. 9.

TABLE 20

Standards of Living in Hong Kong and in China

Item	Percentage of food-expenditure	In China			In Hong Kong
		Sum available (*yüan*)	Price per catty* (*yüan*)	Number of catties obtainable	Number of catties obtainable
Rice . . .	30·76	8·60	0·15	50·6	83·5
Flour . . .	0·17	0·05	0·50	0·1	0·5
Biscuits . .	0·97	0·27	0·94	0·3	1·0
Pork . . .	6·98	1·95	0·70	2·8	2·5
Eggs . . .	1·91	0·53	0·05 †	10 ‡	13 ‡
Vegetable oil .	3·25	0·91	0·60	1·5	2·5
Tea . . .	0·41	0·11	1·50	0·08	0·1

* 1 catty = 1⅓ lb.　　　† per egg.　　　‡ number of eggs.

Source: Szczepanik, *Cost of Living*, p. 13.

Note. As further illustration, two other items can be compared. If, as in Hong Kong, 4·89 per cent. of the total wage is spent on tobacco and cigarettes, the worker in China would buy for 2·53 *yüan* about 169 cigarettes (at 0·30 *yüan* per packet of 20), whereas his Hong Kong counterpart would purchase 420 cigarettes. Again, if the worker in China spends 1·45 per cent. of his wage on soap, he would get 2½ soap cakes (at 0·30 *yüan* per cake) for his 0·75 *yüan*, whereas the Hong Kong worker would be able to buy 2 bars of washing soap and 2 tablets of toilet soap.

TABLE 21

Total Value of Exports of Hong Kong Products, 1955 and 1956
(*HK$*)

Country	1956	1955
Africa, Central (British)	5,482,576	7,386,972
Africa, East (British)	19,854,268	21,748,316
Africa, South	18,932,458	14,861,829
Africa, West (British)	44,382,207	32,569,690
African countries, other	31,210,312	26,994,660
America, Central	12,760,410	10,019,749
America, South (excl. Argentina and Brazil) .	11,828,566	10,809,349
Argentina	4,187	76,586
Asian countries, Central	2,185,454	383,466
Australia	19,331,899	17,679,173
Austria	408	1,800
Belgium	1,894,058	1,662,078
Borneo, North	12,194,546	9,060,078
Brazil	14,622	—
British Commonwealth, other . . .	10,564,556	11,895,417
Burma	6,581,381	11,974,358
Canada	6,627,656	10,219,889
Ceylon	4,336,447	5,504,401
China (excl. Formosa)	4,492,309	42,084
Denmark	1,579,084	1,203,514
Egypt	277,439	507,774
European countries, other . . .	519,725	413,365
Formosa (Taiwan)	1,450,633	664,716
France	660,206	906,596
Germany, Western	2,334,824	1,468,423
India	6,578,871	7,195,590
Indochina	25,132,135	32,291,483
Indonesia	126,023,744	90,286,550
Italy	646,961	658,633
Japan	9,227,923	5,813,349
Korea, South	4,778,869	11,756,676
Macao	4,770,459	6,222,215
Malaya	88,110,591	102,624,203
Middle & Near East countries . . .	11,402,230	9,662,257
Netherlands	3,066,509	1,772,105
New Zealand	5,468,908	6,363,086
Norway	514,335	401,124
Oceania, British	2,685,823	2,517,808
Oceania, United States . . .	3,399,025	3,057,068
Oceania, other	3,386,957	3,521,302
Pakistan	1,696,602	2,271,474
Philippines	24,749,252	18,826,939
Sweden	1,556,408	1,784,446
Switzerland	302,303	364,428
Thailand	48,045,389	60,961,310
Turkey	3,252	37,164
United Kingdom	162,237,778	139,493,657
USA.	20,457,311	15,023,471
West Indies, British	8,851,008	9,357,938
TOTAL	782,592,334	730,318,559

Source: Commerce and Industry Department, *Monthly Report*, December 1956.

TABLE 22

Shipping Statistics, 1939 and 1946–7 to 1955–6
(1947–8 = 100)

Year	Vessels entering and clearing in HK		Tonnage	
	Number	Index	Tons	Index
1939	74,617	135	30,897,948	154
1946–7	46,547	84	13,869,490	69
1947–8	55,344	100	19,969,552	100
1948–9	66,815	121	23,040,126	115
1949–50	63,287	118	27,350,520	136
1950–1	80,792	146	26,844,346	134
1951–2	85,533	154	23,960,207	120
1952–3	77,796	140	23,625,311	118
1953–4	73,602	133	25,846,010	129
1954–5	80,078	145	27,345,059	136
1955–6	87,004	156	28,501,585	142

Source: Marine Department, *Annual Departmental Reports.*

TABLE 23

Post-war Aviation Statistics
(1947–8 = 100)

Year	Numbers and indices of leaving					
	Aircraft		Passengers		Freight (incl. mail)	
	Number	Index	Number	Index	Tons	Index
1940	954	26	6,410	12	320	31
1946–7	1,179	32	12,441	23	125	12
1947–8	3,647	100	54,514	100	1,008	100
1948–9	8,210	225	126,563	232	1,249	124
1949–50	11,016	304	137,431	252	3,266	324
1950–1	2,650	72	41,657	76	1,705	169
1951–2	2,593	71	43,393	80	1,728	171
1952–3	2,592	71	45,899	84	1,802	178
1953–4	2,595	71	52,005	97	1,868	185
1954–5	3,115	85	62,156	114	2,111	210
1955–6	3,503	96	76,791	141	2,513	249

Source: Director of Civil Aviation, *Annual Departmental Reports.*

TABLE 24

Passengers Served by Buses and Trams, 1948–56
(1948 = 100)

Year	HK Tramway Co.		China Motor Bus Co.		Kowloon Motor Bus Co.	
	No. of passengers (million)	Index number	No. of passengers (million)	Index number	No. of passengers (million)	Index number
1948	88	100	20·0	100	56·5	100
1949	109	124	36·0	180	90·0	159
1950	112	127	43·6	218	123·2	218
1951	134	152	46·1	230	145·0	257
1952	134	152	49·2	246	148·5	262
1953	137	156	49·7	248	168·7	299
1954	142	161	47·7	238	172·5	305
1955	146	166	64·5	322	200·0	354
1956	158	180	67·0	335	240·0	425

Source: Hong Kong Annual Reports and information provided by the Companies.

TABLE 25

Services of the Kowloon–Canton Railway, 1946–7 to 1955–6
(1947–8 = 100)

Year	Passenger service			Goods service		
	No. of passengers carried	Passenger-km.		No. of tons carried	Ton-km.	
	Million	Million	Index number	Million	Million	Index number
1946–7	1·9	58·4	67	191·5	6,743	156
1947–8	2·9	86·3	100	122·7	4,308	100
1948–9	3·9	116·2	134	80·1	2,814	65
1949–50	5·3	182·5	211	104·3	3,119	72
1950–1	6·1	152·5	176	371·8	12,885	299
1951–2	3·5	69·5	80	236·9	4,708	109
1952–3	3·6	70·9	82	264·6	5,259	122
1953–4	4·1	111·8	130	174·7	5,835	135
1954–5	3·9	73·2	84	128·8	3,981	92
1955–6	4·0	80·6	93	176·0	6,130	142

Source: General Manager, Kowloon–Canton Railway, *Annual Departmental Reports.*

TABLE 26

Passengers Carried by the Ferries, 1948–56
(million)

Year	Star Ferry	HK. & Y. Ferry	Total	Index of total (1948 = 100)
1948	28	35	63	100
1949	35	42	77	122
1950	37	65	102	162
1951	38	67½	105½	167
1952	36	71	107	170
1953	36	75	111	176
1954	35	75	110	175
1955	35	77	112	177
1956	36	82	118	187

Source: Hong Kong Annual Reports, and information provided by the Companies.

TABLE 27

Post Office Revenue, and Letter Mails and Parcels Received, Dispatched,
and Handled in Transit by G.P.O., 1951–2 to 1955–6

Year	Net revenue (HK$ million)	Letter mails (million)	Parcels
1951–2	6·3	82·2	344,000
1952–3	7·4	98·1	433,000
1953–4	8·5	106·7	601,000
1954–5	10·4	116·1	736,000
1955–6	12·5	125·5	714,207

Source: Postmaster General, *Annual Departmental Reports*. No comparable figures are available for the earlier post-war years.

TABLE 28

Number of Broadcasting Receiving Licences Issued, 1946–56

Year	Number issued	Index (1948 = 100)
1946	12,613	52
1947	13,592	56
1948	24,164	100
1949	33,459	138
1950	42,368	175
1951	43,377	179
1952	41,211	170
1953	42,606	176
1954	41,750	173
1955	52,468	218
1956	58,737	243

Source: Annual Departmental Reports of Postmaster General, *1946–51* and of Public Relations Officer, *1951–6*.

TABLE 29

Consumption of Water, 1946–7 to 1955–6

Year	Consumption in million gallons (rounded figures)	Index (1947–8 = 100)
1946–7	10,500	90
1947–8	11,700	100
1948–9	11,400 *	98
1949–50	12,500 *	107
1950–1	12,200	104
1951–2	12,000	103
1952–3	12,000	103
1953–4	13,500	116
1954–5	10,500	90
1955–6	13,100	112

* Some 200 million gallons are added for the consumption of water in New Territories villages. The official figures for the other years include these villages.

Source: Director of Public Works Department, *Annual Departmental Reports.*

TABLE 30

Gas Manufacture and Distribution, 1947–56

Year	Manufacture & distribution ('ooo cu. ft.)	Index (1948 = 100)
1947	220,344	77
1948	287,468	100
1949	393,308	137
1950	491,415	171
1951	549,130	191
1952	573,211	199
1953	584,726	203
1954	584,806	203
1955	587,011	204
1956	608,068	212

Source: Hong Kong Government Gazette, Supplement no. 4.

TABLE 31

Electricity Charges, 1941, 1946, and 1955
(HK cents per unit)

HK Electric Co.	1941	1946	1955
Light	16	48	15·4–28
Power	5½	16½	11·4–12
China Light & Power Co.			
Kowloon:			
Light	18	71·28	29
Power	7	27·72	14
Cooking/heating . .	5	19·80	13
New Territories:			
Light	—	—	37
Power	—	—	14
Cooking/heating . .	—	—	13

Note: The surcharge, varying with the cost of fuel, which is added to these charges amounted to 9 per cent. in 1955, but was doubled on 1 March 1957 as a result of the closing of the Suez Canal.

TABLE 32

Production of Electricity, 1947–56
('ooo kwh)

Year	Production	Index (1948 = 100)
1947	91,048	61
1948	150,312	100
1949	217,665	145
1950	293,502	195
1951	353,675	235
1952	391,373	260
1953	436,122	290
1954	491,643	327
1955	639,349	426
1956	649,942	433

Source: Hong Kong Government Gazette, Supplement no. 4

TABLE 33

Public and Private Construction, 1948–9 to 1955–6
(HK$ million)

Year	Public construction	Private construction	Total
1948–9	14	70	84
1949–50	19	130	149
1950–1	18	120	138
1951–2	15	68	83
1952–3	40	146	186
1953–4	39	71	110
1954–5	48	90	138
1955–6	86	174	260

Source: Statistics supplied by Rating and Valuation, and Public Works Departments.

TABLE 34

Prices of Building Land, 1954 and 1955
(HK$ per square foot)

Area	1954	1955
Hong Kong Island:		
Banking district	430	500–600
Central business district . . .	200	250
North Point	100	120
West Point	50	70–100
Kennedy Town	40	45
Causeway Bay	30	70
Kowloon:		
Tsimshatsui	130	200
Mongkok	120	130
Shamshuipo & Castle Peak . . .	35–70	90–120

Source: Far East. Econ. R., 24 November 1955, Supplement no. 5, p. 79.

TABLE 35

Basic Wages in the Building and Construction Industry, 1954–5
(HK$ per hour)

Bamboo worker	0·40
Blacksmith I	0·40
Blacksmith II	0·35
Brass fitter	0·40
Bricklayer	0·40
Cabinet-maker	0·40
Carpenter & joiner	0·40
Electrician	0·40
Excavator	0·125
Fitter	0·40
Founder	0·288
Labourer	0·088
Mason	0·40
Painter & glazier	0·40
Paviour	0·288
Plasterer	0·40
Tiler	0·40
Plumber	0·40
Watchman	0·25
Woman labourer	0·075

Source: Interviews.

M

TABLE 36

Manufacture of Chemicals and Chemical Products, March 1955

Product	Number of factories	Employment
Chemicals	8	313
Dyes	4	27
Salt	11	35
Fire crackers	1	275
Fertilizers	1	6
Medicines	18	507
Cosmetics	10	197
Soap	2	18
Paint & lacquer	9	463
Printing ink	3	26
Matches	4	847
Joss sticks & mosquito sticks . . .	10	324
Camphor oil & powder	1	22
Bone-grinding	5	39
Candles	2	42
Lubricating oil	1	3
TOTAL	90	3,144

Source: Commissioner of Labour, *Annual Departmental Report, 1954–5.*

TABLE 37

Number of Factories and Employment in Metal-products Industry,
March 1955

Product	Number of factories	Employment
Enamelware	30	4,658
Tin cans	27	989
Electro-plating	39	962
Hurricane lamps	6	690
Vacuum flasks	6	660
Needles	4	627
Iron & steel ware . . .	8	570
Brass sheets	7	458
Metal windows	11	388
Aluminium ware	6	351
Nails & screws	5	163
Umbrella ribs	2	90
Type-foundries	5	50
Tooth-paste tubes . . .	2	17
Welding	2	9
Other metal wares . . .	176	5,074
TOTAL	336	15,756

Source: Commissioner of Labour, *Annual Departmental Report, 1954–5.*

TABLE 38

Cotton Yarn: Production Capacity, 1955

Mill	Number of spindles	Number of workers employed	Capacity per month in lb. based on 20 counts yarn
East Sun Textile Co. . .	12,528	430	400,000
Eastern Cotton Mills . . .	10,400	350	400,000
Hong Kong Spinners . .	40,240	1,767	1,600,000
Kowloon Textile Industries .	25,600	900	900,000
Lea Tai Textile Co. . . .	10,920	480	440,000
Maryland Textile Co. (HK) .	6,640	150	252,420
Nanyang Cotton Mill . .	29,000	910	1,044,000
New China Textiles . . .	10,800	440	400,000
Overseas Textiles . . .	10,000	300	340,000
Pao Hsing Cotton Mill . .	10,820	455	360,000
Paulum Spinning & Weaving Mills	12,100	395	450,000
South China Textile Co. . .	12,000	440	450,000
South Sea Textile Manufacturing Co.	32,900	1,120	1,170,000
South Textiles	10,080	324	330,000
Star Textiles	17,000	500	500,000
Textile Corporation of Hong Kong	18,168	638	630,000
Wyler Textiles	37,056	1,571	1,565,000
TOTAL	306,252	11,170	11,231,420

Source: Far East. Econ. R., 27 September 1956, p. 408.

TABLE 39

Number of Factories and Employment in Textile Industry,
March 1955

Branch	Number of factories	Employment
Cotton spinning	17	12,402
Wool spinning	1	217
Weaving	148	8,041
Finishing	46	1,187
Knitting mills	295	10,512
Cordage, rope, & twine industries . .	42	838
Other textiles	15	517
Wearing apparel	99	4,261
Made-up textile goods	18	737
TOTAL	681	38,712

Source: Commissioner of Labour, *Annual Departmental Report, 1954–5.*

TABLE 40

Export of Gloves, 1955

	Quantity (m. doz. p.)	Value (HK$ million)
Cotton	1·147	18·34
Woollen	0·929	15·86
Nylon	0·186	3·63
Rayon	0·001	0·02
TOTAL	2·263	37·85

Source: *Trade Bulletin* (Hong Kong), January 1956.

TABLE 41

Number of Factories and Employment in Leather Industry, 1947–55

	Number of factories		Number of employees					
			Male		Female		Total	
	1947	1955	1947	1955	1947	1955	1947	1955
Manufacture of footwear . .	1	12	14	1,024	4	148	18	1,172
Tanneries . .	3	11	107	239	—	6	107	245
TOTAL . .	4	23	121	1,263	4	154	125	1,417

Source: Commissioner of Labour, *Annual Departmental Reports.*

TABLE 42

Dynamic Picture of the Economic Growth of Hong Kong, 1947–8 to 1954–5

	1947–8	*1948–9*	*1949–50*	*1950–1*	*1951–2*	*1952–3*	*1953–4*	*1954–5*
HK $ million:								
Net domestic product at factor cost (current prices) . . .	1,564	1,775	2,330	2,800	2,800	3,200	3,600	4,000
Net domestic product at factor cost (1947–8 prices) . . .	1,564	1,707	2,100	2,300	2,200	2,500	2,800	3,250
Balance of trade (excess of imports over exports) (current prices) . .	424	463	251	254	658	1,010	1,078	1,100
Total government revenue	164	195	264	292	309	385	397	434
Gross real capital formation (current prices) .	95	149	226	183	160	295	234	318
Net real capital formation (current prices) . .	85	133	201	153	124	249	179	250
Index Numbers (1947–8 = 100)								
Net domestic product at factor cost (current prices) . . .	100	113	149	178	177	205	229	256
Net domestic product at factor cost (1947–8 prices) . . .	100	109	134	147	141	148	181	208
Total value of foreign trade	100	135	194	260	247	205	193	187
Total government revenue	100	119	161	178	188	235	242	265
Gross real capital formation (current prices) .	100	156	237	192	168	311	246	335
Gross real capital formation—3 years moving average . . .	—	164	195	199	224	242	297	—
Net capital formation (current prices) . .	100	160	240	180	150	300	210	290
Retail price index . .	100	104	112	121	126	127	126	123
Percentages								
Rate of money income growth (current prices) .	—	+12·5	+28	+18	0	+14	+12	+12
Rate of real income growth (1947–8 prices) . .	—	+ 9	+24	+ 9	− 4	+14	+12	+14
Balance of trade as percentage of national income (*b*) . . .	27	26	11	9	24	31	30	27
Government revenue as percentage of national income . . .	10·5	11	11	10·5	11	12	11	11
Gross rate of real capital formation . . .	6	8·5	10	6·5	6	9	6·5	8·0
Net rate of real capital formation . . .	5·5	7·5	8·5	5·5	4·5	8	5·0	6

Sources: The data for 1947–8 to 1949–50 are based on Ma and Szczepanik, *National Income.* Data for 1950–1 and 1951–2 were prepared by me for a separate publication, and the summary figures have been quoted in the *Economic Survey of Asia and the Far East, 1955,* and reproduced in United Nations, Statistical Office, *Statistics of National Income and Expenditure,* May 1956.

Figures for 1952–3 to 1954–5 are presented here for the first time. They are based partly on the extrapolation of the 1947–52 national-income figures, and partly on the interpolation between the 1951–2 data and the national product data for 1954–5 presented in Table 44; due account being taken of the behaviour of various relevant economic magnitudes between 1952 and 1955.

TABLE 43

Gross Capital Formation Estimates, 1948–9 to 1954–5
(*HK$ million*)

	1948–9	1949–50	1950–1	1951–2	1952–3	1953–4	1954–5
Retained imports of machinery, tools, & equipment .	60·4	70·8	37·2	68·4	99·2	113·4	168·6
Domestic production of machinery, &c. . .	4·8	6·4	8·0	8·8	9·6	10·4	11·0
New buildings & public works	84·0	149·0	138·0	83·0	186·0	110·0	138·0
Total gross capital formation . . .	149·2	226·2	183·2	160·2	294·8	233·8	317·6

Source: Ma and Szczepanik, *National Income* (supplemented by 1954–5 data based on official statistics).

TABLE 44

National Product Estimate, 1954–5

Industrial origin of domestic product	HK$ million	Percentage
Agriculture, forestry, fishing . . .	115	3·0
Mining	15	0·3
Manufacturing	1,300	33·0
Construction	130	3·3
Transportation, communication, utilities .	300	7·5
Wholesale & retail trade . . .	700	17·7
Ownership of dwellings	260	6·5
Public administration & defence . .	340	8·5
Other services	800	20·0
TOTAL	3,960	100·0

Source: Szczepanik, 'An Exercise in the Computation of Hong Kong's National Product', *Far East. Econ. R.*, 22 November 1956. Figures presented in this article were subsequently revised in the light of the analysis carried out in this book.

TABLE 45

Entrepôt Trade

I. *Value of Hong Kong's Imports from Leading Countries, 1948, 1951–6*

(*HK$ million*)

	1948	1951	1952	1953	1954	1955	1956
China (excluding Formosa) . .	430·6	863·1	830·3	857·1	691·8	897·6	1,038·3
Japan . . .	79·1	392·3	482·2	384·1	464·5	526·0	810·6
United Kingdom .	300·9	619·1	470·4	474·4	396·4	441·0	513·3
USA . . .	387·5	373·5	221·1	224·9	281·1	324·9	423·8
Thailand . .	96·2	155·6	204·7	289·8	131·2	185·9	185·4
Malaya . .	84·7	394·1	163·9	177·5	161·6	151·4	152·3
Switzerland . .	40·8	130·9	109·9	105·2	104·6	100·0	131·6
Germany (Western)	4·5 *	214·3	118·9	212·7	155·6	128·4	119·0
Belgium . .	35·1	123·0	70·5	59·8	139·5	97·7	109·3
Australia . .	56·5	88·7	54·8	55·7	63·0	81·5	100·3
Pakistan . .	— †	143·7	90·1	116·4	67·8	53·9	98·0
Netherlands . .	21·7	125·2	108·2	119·2	84·4	64·2	77·9
India . . .	47·5	158·8	100·9	53·5	53·4	83·8	51·0
Formosa (Taiwan) .	— †	62·4	44·7	74·0	46·8	40·3	50·5
Canada . .	36·3	87·9	78·5	58·6	55·1	46·2	46·3
Italy . . .	34·0	125·9	125·6	77·5	31·8	36·6	40·5
Macao . .	89·1	103·6	61·9	66·6	62·3	53·7	40·2
France . .	22·6	123·5	64·1	51·0	33·2	30·9	27·9

* Includes Eastern Germany. † Not separately recorded.

Source: Directory of Commerce, Industry, and Finance, 1957. Throughout Table 45, countries and commodities are ranked according to the value of imports and exports in 1956.

TABLE 45

Entrepôt Trade

II. *Value of Hong Kong's Exports to Leading Countries, 1948,
1951–6*

(*HK$ million*)

	1948	*1951*	*1952*	*1953*	*1954*	*1955*	*1956*
Indonesia . .	68·7	244·8	528·0	372·0	224·6	193·4	501·4
Malaya . .	204·7	740·6	417·6	337·2	330·5	375·4	372·8
Thailand . .	140·2	89·8	243·1	206·7	130·2	179·1	319·6
Japan . . .	49·1	192·5	123·6	221·6	114·7	146·3	318·0
United Kingdom .	75·1	214·6	83·4	119·3	162·2	251·1	298·4
Indochina . .	19·2	34·0	35·2	38·2	50·7	125·6	138·7
China (excluding Formosa) . .	280·5	1,603·8	520·0	540·3	390·8	181·6	136·0
Korea, South .	58·3 *	21·4	22·6	52·5	170·1	192·2	125·2
USA . . .	152·5	162·5	113·5	62·4	70·0	87·9	116·6
West Africa (British)	3·8	12·9	— †	27·3	40·6	53·8	63·9
Macao . .	136·4	228·4	88·9	88·2	63·8	57·4	57·7
African countries, other . .	— ‡	— ‡	35·0	41·8	49·1	55·9	57·1
Australia . .	18·8	72·0	17·5	35·6	46·6	53·4	55·0
Formosa (Taiwan) .	— ‡	139·4	207·4	105·8	79·9	37·4	47·5
Philippines . .	136·4	69·0	45·4	64·0	52·7	53·1	47·0
Burma . . .	12·1	40·9	53·3	39·1	41·3	25·2	31·6
Pakistan . .	— ‡	187·7	55·0	26·4	14·2	5·0	5·3

* Includes North Korea.
† Africa (British): $35·3 million.
‡ Not separately recorded.
Source: As in Table 45 (1).

TABLE 45

Entrepôt Trade

III.   *Principal Imports, 1948, 1951–6*

(*HK$ million*)

	1948	*1951*	*1952*	*1953*	*1954*	*1955*	*1956*
Textiles	353·3	561·0	502·4	454·4	555·2	664·2	921·5
Textile fibres . . .	52·6	312·5	227·1	232·5	259·0	227·3	316·0
Cereals & cereal preparations	145·1	220·4	280·6	371·7	146·7	250·7	275·5
Base metals . . .	100·3	279·9	111·5	115·4	89·7	121·6	265·0
Mineral fuels . . .	118·9	156·1	130·5	112·6	127·6	134·3	207·9
Fruits & vegetables . .	84·7	223·3	239·9	245·7	197·7	200·3	200·1
Animal & vegetable crude materials . . .	57·3	174·3	146·5	168·7	145·1	154·4	176·7
Scientific instruments; photographic & optical goods; watches & clocks . .	43·5	145·7	139·5	159·5	121·6	115·6	165·2
Live animals . . .	33·9	55·4	137·0	110·8	154·3	184·5	162·9
Non-electrical machinery .	55·1	118·7	80·3	94·9	74·7	82·5	122·0
Paper & paperboard .	97·3	171·3	100·1	87·6	97·7	122·3	117·5
Silver, platinum, gems, & jewellery . . .	11·1	27·2	36·1	38·7	42·3	73·3	98·7
Non-metallic mineral-manufactures . .	4·5	11·1	83·8	58·7	54·3	64·2	91·4
Fish & fish preparations .	45·5	79·3	80·3	68·0	60·1	74·8	84·6
Dairy products . .	38·8	96·7	89·4	98·4	86·7	78·3	84·3
Sugar & sugar preparations	47·0	101·3	63·9	115·8	68·0	66·9	83·1
Electrical machinery . .	30·8	86·6	64·4	68·7	48·2	56·8	82·4
Transport equipment .	34·6	70·3	54·0	47·2	46·3	72·1	81·3
Animal & vegetable oils .	103·1	161·8	150·8	133·4	53·3	59·0	78·3
Wood, lumber, & cork .	38·6	88·4	68·0	64·8	56·1	65·4	69·3
Tobacco & tobacco manufactures . . .	51·5	83·4	55·2	58·1	51·5	55·1	59·1
Medicinal & pharmaceutical products . . .	57·1	197·0	148·9	223·0	85·3	47·4	58·3
Coffee, tea, cocoa, & spices	16·0	53·3	51·7	56·2	60·1	57·2	52·9
Chemical elements & compounds . . .	31·0	102·2	132·6	46·4	59·0	52·1	41·8
Dyeing & tanning materials	71·5	167·6	61·0	108·6	128·9	83·3	39·5
Fertilizers . . .	18·4	46·6	—*	44·1	112·5	56·0	37·0

* Less than HK$0·1 million.

Source: As in Table 45 (1).

TABLE 45

Entrepôt Trade

IV. *Principal Exports, 1948, 1951–6*

(*HK$ million*)

	1948	*1951*	*1952*	*1953*	*1954*	*1955*	*1956*
Textiles	326·4	775·7	547·3	462·1	496·0	607·5	835·0
Clothing	55·4	206·9	223·1	223·3	264·8	330·1	399·3
Animal & vegetable crude materials . . .	75·0	206·8	163·8	134·6	140·5	136·9	143·5
Manufactures of metals .	54·4	117·1	122·5	99·0	87·0	104·2	135·4
Fruits & vegetables . .	94·7	175·5	186·3	175·9	129·6	120·3	117·7
Textile fibres . . .	69·1	78·8	61·6	79·6	35·3	41·5	101·2
Footwear . . .	18·2	37·1	26·9	54·9	61·2	81·8	83·7
Plumbing, heating, lighting fittings	26·0	54·6	57·2	45·8	59·9	70·2	78·4
Paper & paperboard .	60·9	155·0	83·6	51·7	53·0	67·7	71·4
Medicinal & pharmaceutical products . .	20·5	228·6	198·7	245·1	110·2	53·4	52·6
Dyeing & tanning materials	41·8	180·1	87·8	121·2	150·8	78·1	51·6
Fertilizers . . .	20·6	62·9	3·1	55·1	111·6	55·8	37·2

Source: As in Table 45 (1).

TABLE 46

Estimates of Net Foreign Investment and of Balance of Payments, 1947–8 to 1954–5

Period	Initial income of period (HK$ million, round figures)	G Rate of income growth (%)	GC (%)	GC-s (%)	b Balance of trade (excess of imports over exports) as a percentage of income	f F as a percentage of income	F Inflow of capital from abroad, plus net balance of invisible earnings, plus net balance of governmental & private transfers (HK$ million)	B Balance of trade (HK$ million)	F Net balance of payments (HK$ million rounded figures)
1947–8 to 1948–9	1,600	12·5	25	15	26·5	41·5	700	443	200
1948–9 to 1949–50	1,800	28	56	46	18·5	64·5	1,200	357	800
1949–50 to 1950–1	2,300	18	36	26	10·0	36·0	800	253	600
1950–1 to 1951–2	2,800	0	0	-10	16·5	6·5	200	456	-300
1951–2 to 1952–3	2,800	14	28	18	27·5	45·5	1,300	834	500
1952–3 to 1953–4	3,200	12	24	14	30·5	44·5	1,400	1,044	400
1953–4 to 1954–5	3,600	12	24	14	28·5	42·5	1,500	1,089	400

Source: Table 42.

Note: In applying the formula: $f = GC - s + b$, the following values were assumed: $C = 2$, $s = 10$ per cent.

The formula is derived from the Harrodian growth equation, $GC = s$, which, if corrected for an open economy, becomes $GC = s - b + f$, where G = rate of income growth, C = capital/output ratio, s = rate of saving, b = balance of trade (excess of imports over exports) as a fraction of income, and f = the sum of the inflow of capital from abroad plus net balance of invisible earnings plus net balance of governmental and private transfers, expressed as a fraction of income.

Index